Interview

Answers to the Top Interview Questions

(Success Tips to Be More Confident & Overcome Anxiety)

Scott Isaacson

Published by Rob Miles

Scott Isaacson

All Rights Reserved

Interview: Answers to the Top Interview Questions (Success Tips to Be More Confident & Overcome Anxiety)

ISBN 978-1-989990-68-1

All rights reserved. No part of this guide may be reproduced in any form without permission in writing from the publisher except in the case of brief quotations embodied in critical articles or reviews.

Legal & Disclaimer

The information contained in this book is not designed to replace or take the place of any form of medicine or professional medical advice. The information in this book has been provided for educational and entertainment purposes only.

The information contained in this book has been compiled from sources deemed reliable, and it is accurate to the best of the Author's knowledge; however, the Author cannot guarantee its accuracy and validity and cannot be held liable for any errors or omissions. Changes are periodically made to this book. You must consult your doctor or get professional medical advice before using any of the suggested remedies, techniques, or information in this book.

Upon using the information contained in this book, you agree to hold harmless the Author from and against any damages, costs, and expenses, including any legal fees potentially resulting from the application of any of the information provided by this guide. This disclaimer applies to any damages or injury caused by the use and application, whether directly or indirectly, of any advice or information presented, whether for breach of contract, tort, negligence, personal injury, criminal intent, or under any other cause of action.

You agree to accept all risks of using the information presented inside this book. You need to consult a professional medical practitioner in order to ensure you are both able and healthy enough to participate in this program.

Table of Contents

INTRODUCTION 1

CHAPTER 1: PREPARATION: THE BEST WAY TO PREPARE FOR AN INTERVIEW 6

CHAPTER 2: ETIQUETTE TIPS FOR YOUR JOB INTERVIEW . 12

CHAPTER 3: STYLES OF INTERVIEWS 16

CHAPTER 4: INTERVIEW MYTHS AND REALITIES 20

CHAPTER 5: HOW TO DRESS FOR MEN AND WOMEN AND OTHER TIPS AND ADVICES 24

CHAPTER 6: THE INTERVIEW PANEL 36

CHAPTER 7: THE PURPOSE OF A RESUME 48

CHAPTER 8: INTERVIEW PREPARATION 55

CHAPTER 9: STAYING CALM DURING THE INTERVIEW 64

CHAPTER 10: WHAT ARE YOUR GREATEST STRENGTHS? . 70

CHAPTER 11: THE TYPICAL INTERVIEW: AN INTRODUCTION TO THE PROCESS 74

CHAPTER 12: WHAT TO INCLUDE 82

CHAPTER 13: MAKING SURE TO HAVE THE RIGHT MINDSET FOR INTERVIEW... 100

CHAPTER 14: WHAT IS YOUR MAXIMUM VALUE? 103

CHAPTER 15: PREPARING FOR PHONE INTERVIEW 107

CHAPTER 16: WHAT IS A JOB INTERVIEW ANYWAY? 111

CHAPTER 17: QUESTIONS ON SALARY, PROMOTION AND BENEFITS 117

CHAPTER 18: YOUR RESUME 129

CHAPTER 19: A GREAT RESUME CAN GET YOU AN INTERVIEW 138

CHAPTER 20: MAKING FIRST IMPRESSIONS 146

CHAPTER 21: CASE QUESTIONS 158

CHAPTER 22: INTERVIEW PARTS 171

CHAPTER 23: THE KEYS TO SUCCESS 178

CHAPTER 24: CLOSING 183

CHAPTER 25: TOP JOB INTERVIEW QUESTIONS 186

CONCLUSION 203

Introduction

The word "Interview" takes us to a new world altogether, which does not only mean sitting in front of the interviewer and confidently presenting yourself but also selling your skills and knowledge (and also experience in case you have already worked before) in the calmest and composed manner. Interview as a concept is like an adrenaline rush which brings with itself a lot of excitement and a ray of hope to start working (again) in a new organization, with new people from different backgrounds and taking control of your life in your hands without having to depend on anybody else, and most importantly an improved standard of living making you an aware and professionally intellectual person with a completely new skill set ready to unflare them in the practical world.

An interview is an essential process for every company that requires hiring employees. It is an interactive process where both parties connect with each other's personalities. It is a two-way communication process where the employer asks questions from the candidate, not necessarily to get an answer but to judge their absolute power, speaking skills, personality, and attitude. Other traits like 'body language' speak a lot-even when the candidate tries to hide some of his habits, to get selected. Hence it becomes crucial for the candidate not to conceal these traits and habits but to reshape and transform your personality and attitude in a positive way. Similarly, the interviewee tries to connect with his interviewer positively and decides to ask him relevant questions about work.

An interview is necessary as an employer would never want to hire a candidate who is not deserving enough for that position. The interviewer correctly judges the academic qualifications, skills, and experiences, and personality of the candidate and after that, announces the result. Hence, the interviewee must prepare for his job interview preparation tips thoroughly. Nowadays, there has been a lot of competition in terms of employment, which further makes the selection and hiring process more difficult. So to get selected for your dream job, you have to work hard right from the start to the end. You have to work hard not only on your physical appearance but your spoken skills, your attitude, and personality.

It is not easy for everyone to crack their dream job interviews easily. Sometimes even the most proficient people are rejected due to one reason or the other. This failure may reduce your confidence and positivity. You may feel incapable of achieving what you want. In this case, you have to work on your weaknesses and build them strong, instead of criticizing yourself.

Therefore, "doing your homework" as it is said becomes a significant step towards interview success. This means preparing yourself for the interview entirely. This is a broad concept which includes:

Knowing about the history of the organization to the business hierarchy to its current market position.

Being well informed about the role and responsibilities of the job position you are applying for.

If it is your first interview ever or you have worked before, make sure you do not sound or appear desperate or nervous or over-confident at all.

Instant Interview Success is not a myth. There are a lot of things that might make or break the interview you appear for. It's not necessary that you might be or have to be rejected in a couple of interviews only; that's when you learn how to appear in an interview.

There is no set or pre-designed criteria to be followed for an interview success as well. The key to interview success always lies with you, the one appearing for the interview. We should not forget that the interviewer is a human being as well, and they are here to hire you, so being real and honest to yourself is the best.

The best part in an interview is when the interviewer (s) like you, they stop pushing you to do well often unknowingly, by explaining the questions or elaborating the situations more fully, helping you along when you are searching for a word or an example to answer that particular question. This emphasis on people skills is done to underline how people skills can give an interviewee an edge over another.

Chapter 1: Preparation: The Best Way To Prepare For An Interview

Take a Good Look at Yourself

This is meant in a figurative and literal manner. Don't just make sure that you look good for your interview. Sounding good is more important. You need to present yourself as a person of substance and skill. How is that done?

Start with your CV. This is the first document that your target company will see coming from you. This is the first thing you have to master; because what good is an employee who can't remember their own qualifications and work history?

Take a good look at what you have accomplished and memorize your work history. Ask someone to help quiz you on your history. Nothing could be more embarrassing than asking for your CV back from your interviewer because you forgot something on it.

Understand the Job Description and Requirements

If you have a copy of the job/wanted ad, go over it again with the intent of studying it. If it's an online application, visit the online portal of the company to which you're applying and take a look at the vacancy.

What you're looking for are important details about the opening they have. Besides knowing the position, you also need to remember what kind of qualities and skills the company needs. Here are some examples:

Above average communication skills

Self-Supervised

Willing to work in a team

These may sound like easy statements to remember, but the trick here is to incorporate these prerequisites into your answers. This information will come in handy especially when answering tough questions like "why should we hire you?" There will be more explanations on this particular question later on within this book.

Studying these requirements and skills will also help you determine if you're a good fit for the job yourself. You may be qualified but might end up uncomfortable in your chosen job.

Get to know Your Would-Be Employer

A common mistake that a lot of applicants make is to just look at the wanted ad and immediately send in their application. As mentioned earlier, doing your homework is very important and it doesn't stop with studying the job requirements.

Take it another step further by studying the company/business in question. On top of getting a better appreciation for your soon-to-be-employer, you will also have a better chance acing the interview.

First, start with the history of the company. Where did it start? Who are the heads? How did the company reach its current position? Has the company recently held any celebrations for any milestone achievements?

Although those things may sound irrelevant to your job application, showing your interviewer that you've done your homework on them will surely be a plus side. Showing them that you are interested in their history means that you take them (and the job) very seriously.

Besides looking at the history and background of the company, another important item to look for is the Mission/Vision Statement.

This handy piece of literature is very important for any company. This is because the Mission/Vision Statements represent the very core of your prospective company.

The Vision Statement reflects how the company sees itself. Do they envision themselves as the leading provider of a particular service? Do they aim to become a global presence in the next few years? Are they aiming to become the top distributor/service provider in the continent? Whatever those goals are as a company, it will be part of the Vision Statement.

On the other hand, the Mission Statement talks about how the company will achieve their goals. Shall they focus on catering to customer needs? Will they offer reliable and refundable services to their clientele? Who will these clientele be? This information is available from the Mission Statement.

It may sound strange to be studying these things for a job interview but the advantage this information will bring you is indispensable. If you really want to impress your interviewer, show them that you took the time to know the company and you've understood just exactly what the company is trying to accomplish as a whole.

One final thing that you need to review are the company core values. This is a simple collection of attitudes/values that the company deems vital to their success. It goes without saying that if you want to work for that particular company, it's required that you exhibit those values as well.

These values could be anything from honesty, integrity, cooperation, wisdom, stewardship and the like. Although they sound like mother-goose statements, they should come in handy when it comes to answering interview questions in this manner:

"You should hire me because I understand that your company prides honesty above all else. This is why the company envisions itself as the number one service provider in the market. I also take honesty and integrity quite seriously."

Chapter 2: Etiquette Tips For Your Job Interview

Etiquette is the way you conduct yourself in a business environment. Knowing proper interview etiquette for your job interview to be successful is very important. Job interview etiquettes include your dress code, mode of communication with your interview, things you bring to an interview and courtesy around your interviewer, etc.

To win your desired job, you must consider all the nooks and crannies of your job interview etiquettes

1. Dress code on a job interview

Your dress code to an interview is as important as preparing yourself for interview questions and answers. Your appearance makes the first impression about you to your interviewer, so you should dress responsibly avoiding clothing that is too tight, exposes your body parts or offensive combination of colors. Dress code is essential for acquiring a professional position.

2.Things you should bring to a job interview

What you bring to a job interview is vital as it shows how prepared you are for the position. Paying attention to details like extra copies of your CV with a list of references and also proofs of previous jobs done or places you have worked before. Also, ensure to bring some tools to operate with depending on your area of specialization, e.g. a laptop for a tech job.

3.Simple courtesy around your interviewer

You should act according to courtesy in your interview location at all times as you never can tell who you might be talking with. Speak politely to the receptionist on your arrival and inform them of your appointment. Greet your interviewer with a firm handshake followed by an introduction and ensure to follow his conversation guide correctly.

4. How to respond to interview questions

At this point, applying good listening skills is very important. Listen to the questions attentively, avoid talking when your interviewer is talking, ask for a repeat if you didn't get the question and give a correct and precise response. Avoid digressions or repetitions when answering questions, answer in time, and be sure of your response for this is your opportunity to impress your interviewers with your answers.

5. Closing the interview

At this point, you should create a good impression about your interest. Let the interviewer know you are the perfect fit for the job, and you are very much interested. Proceed to ask about their hiring process and when you might expect to hear from them, but avoid being too forward. Lastly, thank them for the opportunity and time spent interviewing you.

Chapter 3: Styles Of Interviews

There is more than one style of job interview. One is what's considered a normal interview. Just you and the hiring supervisor.

Smaller companies and businesses usually only have one or two people involved in asking you questions during your interview. The immediate supervisor is one.

Once you make it past the immediate supervisor usually the owner or main manager of the company will give a final interview.

Sometimes you are told on the spot you have the job. Other times they will say they will be in touch. I'd much rather know before I leave but it's a cruel world sometimes.

Larger companies and businesses may use the normal above method or a group interview. Also known as a panel interview. If you have never had this type of interview don't let the description "group or panel" frighten you away from trying to get a new job or a promotion that you deserve. Usually a group interview has 3 to 6 people in the room with you asking you questions.

I read online in my research that Apple computers, Google, large banks, Amazon, hospitals use group interviews.

There are times that a group interview also means you are not the only candidate for the job being asked some questions. They may have several job seekers all together at the same table.

Keep in mind you may not all be interviewing for the same position. You may even be asked to participate in a small group activity together with the other candidates. This is so you can demonstrate if you work well as a team player or if you are more of an individual worker, rather than excelling in a group or on a team.

Usually employers want you to be a team player and at times be able to work alone unsupervised. It's a balancing act, but you can do it. Have faith and your self-confidence will radiate from you.

It is important to speak up during a group interview. If you say nothing you will fade in the background unnoticed. The other side of that coin is do not monopolize the conversation. You don't want to come across as arrogant or pushy. Sometimes let others answer a question even if you know the answer.

It is also good if at least once you compliment an answer from one of the other candidates. It won't sabotage you to say something like, "Good point, Sam" This shows you are listening to the others, working as a team. Don't get carried away with that, once is probably enough.

In a group interview your actions as well as your answers are being observed. Be mindful of your body language. Don't cross your arms over your chest. That is a closed off position. Of course, never pick your nose. Just kidding I know you only do that in private. You get my meaning I am sure.

Now let's move on to chapter three where I am sharing ideas about things for you to do in preparation before the interview.

Chapter 4: Interview Myths And Realities

For many applicants, job interviewing seems to take place within a big black box. It is shrouded in mystery and apprehension. You don't know what will transpire until you go inside an office to meet an interviewer to discuss the situation. In the meantime, many job hunters can only guess what the interview will be like.

They worry about how they should dress, what they should say, when and how to talk about salary, how to close the interview, and if and when it's appropriate to follow-up the interview with a telephone call. Most aspects of job interviewing are surrounded by myths that contribute to interviewing apprehension. These myths prevent many individuals from properly preparing for the interview. In this chapter, we address four of the most common interview myths as well as outline the realities for each. By examining each myth, you should be better prepared for the realities of the job interview - getting the job.

2.1 Myth 1

My resume will get me the job.

REALITY: Your resume helps communicate your qualifications to employers. Resumes are used to screen candidates and select those to interview. Few people ever get hired on the basis of their resume. Over 95% of employers hire on the basis of a personal interview.

2.2 Myth 2

Invitations to interviews normally come by letter or fax.

REALITY: Most employers issue invitations to interview by telephone. In fact, many interviewers will telephone you in order to conduct a screening interview over the phone. Based on how well you do in this interview, you will be invited by telephone to attend a formal job interview.

Therefore, you should be well prepared to handle this telephone screening interview.

2.3 Myth 3

I will get invited to an interview based on the quality of the information found in my resume, letters, and applications.

REALITY: Invitations to interview come from many different sources. Resumes, letters, and applications are important screening devices, but they are by no means the only ones nor the most important. These sources primarily demonstrate qualifications and capabilities in written form. Since most jobs are intensely interpersonal, interviewers also seek verbal and interpersonal sources of information about candidates before inviting them to interview.

2.4 Myth 4

Once I submit my application for a job, the proper thing to do is to wait until I hear from the employer.

REALITY: It is perfectly acceptable to call the employer within two weeks of submitting your written materials to ask when you might expect to hear about the selection of candidates to be interviewed. Employers often fail to inform candidates whether or not they are still under consideration. It is to your advantage to get a definite "yes" or "no" rather than waste your time doing nothing else in anticipation of being called for an interview.

Chapter 5: How To Dress For Men And Women And Other Tips And Advices

The big day has finally arrived. You've done your homework; you're ready for that hiring manager. With any luck, you went to bed early and got a good night's sleep, knowing you're well prepared for the following day. You get up early, allowing yourself ample time for breakfast. If you have more than one interview, you may want to carry a snack to pump up your energy. This is a day when you need to be alert and focused, confident, and prepared.

How to Dress for Success

As superficial as it sounds, employers will judge you on the way you are dressed. This does not mean that if you wear anything less than Prada the job will go to someone else. It simply means that the interviewer looks at your exterior as a representation of your interior. If it is obvious that you took the time to choose the right clothes for this interview, it is likely that you will put the same amount of thought into your work. Arriving for an interview too casually dressed tells the interviewer that you don't care enough about the job or the company to put your best self forward. Dress up a little bit more for your interview than you would if you were actually going to work at the company. The Outfit

Your physical appearance is very important for you to prepare for because "first impressions" matter so much. When you look the part and they appreciate what you have presented to them, you have a better chance of landing the position. Understand that although appearances are merely superficial, they matter greatly because it is part of your personal branding and image.

Make Sure that Your Clothes Are Properly Cleaned and Pressed

Try on your outfit ahead of time to make sure that everything fits and that you look great wearing them. Do not make a mistake of putting off until to the night before or the day of the interview because you may not have time to make adjustments if necessary

Plan in advance for the right accessories and shoes to wear with the outfit, making sure it is appropriate and not too dressy or casual for the office. See how you look when you are sitting down because the interview will be with you sitting on a chair in front of the interviewer

Grooming. Get a haircut if it is long overdue and make sure to come properly groomed, so that you give out a good first impression.

Dressing up for an interview can be tricky. Always it is going to be important for you to match your outfit to what the people in the company wear but if you have no idea what to wear, just keep it formal or go a notch higher. A business suit is always the safest choice. It will be harder for you to go wrong with this so stick to the basics. The rules of dress laid out below for both men and women are very specific and should be strictly followed. Though the lines between what men and women can and do wear to work on a regular basis are becoming more and more blurred—khakis and a button-down shirt can work well on either of the sexes—there are two definite sets of rules during the job interview process.

For Men

If you are a man interviewing for a professional position, you should always wear a suit. A shirt and tie might be sufficient to make you the best-dressed guy at your current job, but it won't cut it in an interview. More conservative colors—black, navy blue, or charcoal gray—are the best colors to choose. Bright and flashy colors will only serve to distract the interviewer from what you are saying. For men, the tie has become one of the few creative outlets when it comes to dressing professionally. A bad choice in the neckwear department can spell almost certain doom. A solid dark color with tiny geometric patterns is the safest bet.

You can change the look of a conservative colored suit dramatically by changing the tie, the shirt, or both. If you only have one suit, these changes can help you out tremendously when you're interviewing with companies that require two or more meetings on separate occasions. Avoid shiny shirts; they are a major no-no and should be reserved for the nightclub scene. Socks should blend in well with the shoes and pants.

For Women

The rules of proper workplace attire for women have been changing over the past several decades. The power suit that once ruled the scene has been replaced with the traditional pantsuit that doesn't differ much from the men's version. Pants for women have now become widely accepted and may be particularly appropriate in settings where you may be doing a lot of walking or getting in and out of cars. If wearing a skirt, the length of the skirt, obviously, should be tasteful and professional. Knee length is always appropriate. Again, regardless of the company's particular dress code, women, too, are expected to wear a suit to the interview.

One detail not to overlook: your shoes. Interviewers often gauge a candidate by his shoes—are they worn, polished, fashionable? While it is something a candidate might neglect, it's a very telling detail for the interviewer and one that might cost the candidate a job. Colors should be conservative. A black or navy blue skirt/pants and jacket is the best choice. Avoid colors like pink and powder blue—they won't help you assert your professionalism. Don't wear anything that dangles. That goes for earrings, bracelets, and necklaces. Avoid clothes that are too tight; you'll be less comfortable and you won't be taken as seriously.

Grooming

Personal grooming is definately another matter that each candidate must attend and focus no before stepping out of the door to attend an interview. Careful grooming is one thing that indicates both self-confidence and thoroughness. Women must remember not wear jewelry or excessive makeup. If you have your nails painted, make sure they are of an official conservative color, simply look like a professional.

Men should be sure to check that any facial hair is neat and trim. If you have a beard or a mustache, make sure it is well groomed. Otherwise, men should make sure that they are clean-shaven when they arrive for an interview. If your five o'clock shadow comes at three o'clock and your interview is at four, make sure you have time to run home quickly and shave.

There are advantages to scheduling a few interviews in one day. For one, you'll already be decked out in your interviewing gear, and your briefcase or bag will be stocked with the essential spare resume, work samples, and reference sheets. Some people find they get into a mental zone after one interview that lets them gear up for additional interviews.

All candidates should wear very little—if any—perfume or cologne. Cigarette-scented clothing may also offend an interviewer with a sensitive nose. Remove any nose rings, cover your tattoos with long sleeves, and tuck your water bottle in your briefcase, not a knapsack.

The Resume

The resume is passed beforehand and chances are, it is the reason why you landed the interview in the first place. If the employer likes what he saw in your resume, he will call you for an interview. When you come in, you have to make sure you know your resume by heart. You prepared it, he expects you to know it and he should be able to question you about the details of your educational and work experience.

It does not matter if you held that position years ago, refresh yourself of the details of the job so that you can answer inquiries about it.

The Company

It is also very important that you know about the company and the very position you are interviewing for. You can do online research so that you can find out the business/office structure and learn the names of the people that run it. Find out more about the company and study its history, mission and vision so that you can engage in a knowledgeable conversation with the interviewer.

Interviewers appreciate it when it shows that you took the time to know the company. It will motivate you to ask intelligent questions as well.

The Location

Familiarize yourself with the location of the interview and if you are unsure about it, it may be worth doing an ocular visit prior to the day of the interview so that you can arrive early and not waste your time getting lost. If you need to print a map, do so, because it will guide you well.

Arriving late is not going to be good at all because it leads them to make assumptions about you. If you arrive late, they could assume you are a perpetually tardy person even if you did not mean to be late. An ocular visit, as advised, would help you time the journey so that you can leave at the right hour and arrive at the office with enough time to prep yourself and freshen up.

Pre-Interview Preparations

Chances are good that the person who invites you in for an interview will also offer to give you directions to the building. Take these directions! Even if you have a good idea of the location of the company, you'll want to know exactly where you are going.

If you are unfamiliar with the area, it might be a good idea to drive to the company before you actually have to meet for the interview. Map out the directions and time how long it will take for you to get there. If possible, do a test run to see how long the trip might take and to make sure you know where you're going. Even if you have access to a GPS, getting specifics from the individual you will be interviewing with will provide you with a solid backup and details that a GPS may not be able to convey such as where to park, which door to enter, etc.

Before you go out the door, make sure you have the following items:

•Resume

•Cover letter

- Writing implement
- Spare tie or pair of nylons
- List of professional references
- Driver's license and social security card

Add a few extra minutes for traffic or any other unforeseen delays. Plan to arrive for the interview at least ten to fifteen minutes early.

When scheduling your interview, be sure you know the name of the person you will be meeting with. The person who calls to screen you over the phone is not always the same person you'll be interviewing with. Find out the person's name, title, and phone number. Enter the phone number and contact information into your cell phone for easy access. That way, if a problem arises, you can contact this person directly.

Chapter 6: The Interview Panel

There are five main types of interview formats.

Different types of interview panel:

Telephone Interview – you will be interviewed by one person.

1-1 Interview – you will be interviewed probably by the person you will directly report to.

Sequential Interview – you will be interviewed in two or more phases on the same day and each interview will be either 1-1 or 1-2.

Panel Interview – you will be interviewed by three or more people who will be led by a chairperson.

Group Interview – you will be interacting with other candidates shortlisted for the role and you will be assessed on your performance as part of the group.

Panel Members

When you accept the interview invitation ask who you will be meeting and the format the interview will take. Any agency or HR department will be happy to give you this information if you request it, it shows initiative and your interest in the job. Ask for their names, their position at the company and what their role is during the interview.

Find out what you can the members of the panel; about their current position and how it relates to the role you are applying for. Look at their career history, sources you can use include LinkedIn, Company People Profiles, Google and your local Library may have other resources available. Then consider what types of questions each person is likely to ask.

How long have they been with the company? If they have been employed with this company for more than 10 years does this mean the company has a policy of promoting from within?

Does the Interviewer have direct work experience of the role you are applying for? Could they be the person leaving the role you are applying for?

Company Research

Questions probing your knowledge about the company are common in interviews, particularly when companies are recruiting for graduate jobs. If you can demonstrate your knowledge about the basic details of the company, it will show you have prepared for the interview and done your research.

There are lots of sources of company information for you to put together a well-rounded profile of the company.

Start with the company website. It contains a huge amount of information about the company. This is the platform they use to promote themselves and how they want their customers and the market to perceive them. The messages and information they share this way will have consistent messages and you will be able to get a sense of their goals, ethos and how they see their position within their industry.

Having read about the company from their perspective it is useful to read a few objective opinions, information that will allow you to form a more balanced view. News services such as Google News, BBC and Bloomberg, for example, will likely be reporting on the noteworthy issues affecting the company. Significant events such as these impact the company and will be of interest to companies and people operating in the sector so would be covered by the news services:

Awards & Intl Recognition

Mergers & Acquisitions

Changes in Leadership

Corporate Events – good or controversial

Summarise the information you have found into bullet points or short paragraphs so it will be useful. As you interview approaches it will be a useful refresher for your memory on all the information you have read. Your summary may include these items;

Company name

Directors – names and positions

Interview panel – names and position

Business Activities – what sort of industry & where are they active

Historic – when they established, how have they developed, have there been any significant events in their recent history

Future – what are their plans, in the next 5 years and longer-term

Have there been recent announcements which are relevant to the role you are applying for

Topics most discussed/reported in industry news, in the last 6mths, 1year, 3years.

Any changes in the regulatory environment that are impacting the industry.4

Industry commentary opinion on the impact of the changes

Prepare questions

Prepare specific questions for the interview panel about the company, the role, their expectations and where they see the opportunity for you. Make notes of the questions that come to mind as you research so that you can come back to them later.

Put yourself in the role of the interviewer and imagine what questions you would ask a candidate. Start with the job specification for each point and write down the questions you would ask a person applying for this role. Be impartial when identifying possible questions, the more realistic your questions will be, and you will end up with a set of questions some of which will challenge you.

Referencing the job description write interview questions for each of the following sections and items:

Experience – these questions will ask for examples of experiences from your career

o   Talk us through your CV

o   Tell us about your role at …

o   What was your experience of …

Technical – these questions will focus on your technical knowledge and experience

o   How did you manage project …

o   How would you do …

o   Can you create … describe how …

Competency – these questions will relate to specific items in the job description o Leadership responsibilities, eg. describe a time when you successfully dealt with conflict within a team.

o Stakeholder management, eg. how would you manage stakeholder expectations in time-critical situations?

o Financial responsibilities, eg. how do you develop a financial forecast.?

Character – these questions are designed for you to show how you would manage in specific situations

o Describe a difficult situation and how you overcame it?

o What are your strengths and weaknesses?

o What achievement are you most proud of?

Practice Interview

Once you've thought about all the questions that could be asked for each of the items on the job description you need to switch gears and put yourself back in your shoes and think about how you will answer all those questions.

Try to keep your answers concise and relevant, think about what you would say if you had to write your answers on the back of a postcard, make sure that you answer the question that has been asked.

Focus on the points that demonstrate your strengths and experience especially where that is documented in your CV. When possible answer strategically – does the question relate to company strategy? If so, you may want to note this in your answer. Can you talk about any gains or losses/pitfalls based on your experience? Are there known industry issues you would need to allow for or workaround.

Questions for the Interview Panel

Interviews are a two-way process and just as important as the questions that the interviewers ask are the questions you choose to ask them. There will be an opportunity at the end of the interview for you to ask questions. Use this opportunity to probe for extra detail that isn't on the job description, about the team or the company.

Try to keep your questions to a maximum of three and focused on specific topics, prepare follow-up questions as well in case the interviewer doesn't quite answer the question you have asked. If you have asked your questions as the interview has progressed, try to rephrase them and summarise the key points you have covered during the interview. Bear in mind, if the questions you ask at the end of your interview relate to salary or holiday allowance it doesn't demonstrate your interest in the role or engagement with your career so the panel may not consider you as seriously as you would prefer.

Some stock questions you could ask might be;

What are your short, medium and long-term targets for the person you select for this role? What would you like the candidate to accomplish in the first 30 or 90 days?

What sort of training and development programmes does the company run? Do you use any external training providers, if YES for what?

Are there opportunities to work with teams outside of my core responsibilities on cross-functional projects? What sort of projects has there been in this area in the past?

You can ask questions that challenge the interviewer to reflect on your interview performance and give you a final opportunity to influence their decision, hopefully in your favour. But, if you ask one of these questions be prepared to be able to speak positively about your suitability and convince them you are the right candidate for this job.

Is there anything we've discussed that would give you concerns over employing me?

Are there any skills or experience you feel I'm missing?

Chapter 7: The Purpose Of A Resume

Six seconds. That is how long, on average, hiring managers and recruiters spend looking at a resume before deciding whether to discard the applicant. If your resume does not grab attention quickly and compel the reader to look closer, it is not doing its job — and your job hunt will suffer. Unfortunately, much of the advice offered to resume writers tends to focus on the applicant, not the person reading the document and his or her short attention span. In some ways, this makes sense; after all, the resume is, on the surface, about you and your history. Realistically, the resume's greater purpose is to show potential employers what you can do for their companies, not advertise the simple fact that you are amazing.

To help move you from the mindset of a resume writer to that of a person in charge of hiring, consider the following three facts about how HR departments handle resumes. With each one, you'll be given suggestions on how you can avoid the standard resume mistakes and instead provide information in a manner that will cause you to stand out as an interview candidate. Once you understand the resume-writing attitude you need to cultivate, you'll be ready to move to the next chapter, select the type of resume, and begin writing.

Fact No. 1: Those in charge of hiring do not read resumes — they scan resumes

Resume writers are often encouraged to craft their documents with consistency from start to finish so that it looks good under scrutiny. Using this method, each section of the work is balanced in tone and length, eventually creating a well-rounded picture of the individual as a professional. This tactic would work if those reviewing resumes read them from start to finish carefully, but studies have shown again and again that this is not the way resumes are handled in real life. Those reading resumes scan, usually quickly. To be successful, the document should contain tantalizing, eye-grabbing tidbits of information backed by evidence that ultimately causes the reader to want to pick up the phone and speak to the applicant.

Crafting a resume with information that grabs the eye, fortunately, isn't too difficult. The most pertinent information under each category should be prominently displayed in the shortest, most action-oriented way possible so that the reader is encouraged to look more closely at the details. So, for example, the lead sentence under a teacher's objective might read: "To hold an elementary math teaching position at a school that values dedication, student engagement, and professional development." The person reading quickly understands the type of position the applicant wants and the career areas he or she values, making it easy to assess whether the candidate warrants further consideration.

Compare this to an objective for the same position: "I would like to work in a position as an elementary school teacher. I think professional development is important, and I think the school I work for should, too. I would be best suited for teaching math." Because there are too many superfluous words and the information is needlessly spread out over many sentences, the recruiter is not seduced into reading more — potentially landing the resume in the rejection pile.

Fact No. 2: There's no guarantee a human will read your resume

Typical resume-writing advice also doesn't take into account the way many companies handle resumes in the 21st century. Instead of being looked at by the hiring manager, resumes are entered into a database, one which a hiring manager can search by keywords. The eye-grabbing parts of your resume, then, should do double duty by containing keywords related to what the company is likely to be looking for.

The most effective way to ensure that the hiring manager will come across your resume is to customize your resume for each company you apply to. You can often gain an idea of what recruiters are likely to be searching for simply by reading job ads thoroughly. A company that needs "a reliable, down-to-earth agent to help families with their insurance needs" is probably not going to be searching for buzzwords like "dynamic" or "synergy." By subtly altering the language you use in your resume to match the job ad, you'll be increasing the chances that your resume will be pulled. After all, it is highly possible that the people who wrote the ads are also doing the searching, and they've already told you what they are looking for.

Fact No. 3: The best candidate does not always get the interview

It is not uncommon for one open position to garner several hundred responses. Because the individual reviewing the resumes is often scanning, as noted previously, he or she can easily skip right past the most-qualified candidate if that candidate has a long, unappealing, or less-than-user-friendly resume. However, this is good news for job applicants who understand how to make their credentials pop off the page. This can put them above co-applicants who haven't done so, even if these co-applicants have better credentials.

The tricks here is to identify exactly what the person is reading the resume is looking for, and then place it as close to the top of the resume as possible, still conveying the information in the shortest, most-action-oriented way possible. If you are applying to a job that requires a degree in electrical engineering, don't hide this information on the second page or in small print at the bottom of the first. Make sure that the education section is quickly identifiable and clearly features the information the reader is scanning for. Related qualifications or skills that can help your chances should be handled in the same manner. Remember, resume reviewers probably won't take the time to search your document for what they need; make it so easy for them to find the information that they cannot miss it.

Ultimately, your resume is an advertisement of you and your skills. Ask yourself which you would rather have — a Super Bowl ad meticulously designed to delight viewers or a low budget, hastily produced ad on public access television? To get the elite feeling of a Super Bowl ad for your resume, you do not need to spend a fortune. Take the time to think about the people who will be on the receiving end of your ad, consider their needs and what will grab their attention, and you'll be on your way to success.

Chapter 8: Interview Preparation

Preparing a job interview is very fraught or traumatic. A job interview is one of the most drawn out and intimidating ways of making first impression. Even if you have less than a day before your job interview, you can outshine the competition with a little interview preparation.

Get your closet all together and give yourself more travel time than you might suspect you may need. VISUALIZE the meeting.

Picture yourself as balanced, certain, eloquent.

Make a list of your qualities and practice how you will explain them.

Write out responses to the inquiries you would prefer not to be inquired. It will help ease you nervousness.

The prior minutes before you go out for that difficult task meeting, may not contain the same level of power, but rather mental arrangement can still mean the distinction between triumph(landing the position) and annihilation(back to classifieds).

Specialist suggests that employment seekers visualize in their minds how the interview will go. A little restlessness before a meeting can be useful in the event that it makes you ready and stimulated, yet an excessive amount of tension can be awful. Rehearsing profound breathing or repeating a tranquil word like "calm" are well known techniques individual utilization to get themselves ready for a tense stimulation. And, again, mental preparation well in advance of an interview is the key thing.

To gain confidence, official mentors advice you write down a few regarding your most prominent achievements and afterward list the abilities you used to accomplish them. On the off chance that you know your abilities and how you make a difference, it will be less demanding to discuss them in a meeting setting.

The same rationale applies to your shortcomings. Much sooner than the day of the meeting, competitors ought to consider strong responses to three inquiries they would prefer not to be inquired. Record them in the event that you need to and go over them a few times. This will go far toward soothing uneasiness.

What's more, shouldn't something be said about everybody's most despised inquiry— how old would you say you are? Most questioners are sufficiently adroit to know it's unlawful to straightforwardly ask, yet regularly you'll get an inquiry, for example, "What year did you move on from school?" that by implication tests at your age. On the off chance that you come clean, the questioner then knows your age and may not have any desire to contract you in view of it. On the off chance that you say you would prefer not to answer the inquiry, you could run over ineffectively and may make the questioner uncomfortable.

Here's how you can finesse the situation. To begin with, accept the questioner doesn't have ulterior thought processes. Instead, figure that he or she is trying to learn something, albeit clumsily, about your ability to do the job. So listen to the inquiry, and then ask your own particular question consequently to focus the questioner's basic motivation.

For instance, you could respond, "I'm interested to know why you are asking me this. Are you stressed that my abilities may be obsolete?" or "That is a fascinating inquiry. Are you examining to find out about the relevance of my aptitudes or my course work?" The interviewer should then respond with the reason for the question, which allows you to say something good about yourself. Frame your response as a showcase of what you've learned and prove that your training is current.

Pre-interview appraisal tests are another wellspring of uneasiness– or inconvenience– for some heading into a meeting. Hopefuls ought to consider the appraisals important, regardless of the possibility that they feel they aren't essential. Furthermore, clear your timetable. Get some information about to what extent a pre-employment evaluation may take, as you may need to give anyplace from a couple of minutes to a few hours of your time. You can likewise acquaint yourself with pre-employment appraisals by taking free ones on the Web, for example, online test Inc., a pre-employment testing and evaluation organization in Atlanta. Practice tests can help you feel greater for when it's your turn in the last place anyone would want to be.

Knowing you looks awesome for a meeting makes certainty also. Make sure to get that suit squeezed well ahead of time of the huge day, soften up your shoes and don't run over the edge with garish extras or architect touches. Feeling surged or stressing you may be late can divert from your magic, as well, so it's a smart thought to give yourself more travel time than you might suspect you require.

Generally, before a major meeting, mental and vocation specialists concur that it's essential to concentrate on the positive. The main thing is that you should continuously consider, discuss, and rehearse precisely what you need to hap.

The greatest oversight in meeting is not being completely arranged. It profits work seekers to utilize each possible means conceivable to get ready for the meeting and to permit plentiful time to completely plan. Comprehend that talking is ability; as with all abilities, readiness and practice improve the nature of that aptitude.

Readiness can have the effect between getting an offer and getting rejected.

There is nobody "best" approach to plan for a meeting. Maybe, there are particular and vital systems to improve one's chances for meeting achievement. Each meeting is a learning background, so discovering that happens amid the readiness and genuine meeting procedure is helpful for future meetings.

Beginning arrangement requires late appraisal of abilities, intrigues, qualities, and achievements; a re-evaluation and redesigning of one's resume; and research on the focused on organization/association and position. Readiness likewise incorporates genuine routine of run of the mill and focused on inquiries questions. Last arrangement incorporates points of interest of dress and appearance, learning of the area of the meeting, what's in store, and conventions for follow up.

Select suitable clothing much sooner than the meeting day. Know the way of life of the association for which you are meeting and dress as needs be - maybe a score over that - particularly if the organization has embraced corporate easy going. A matching suit is constantly adequate. Be sure that your garments are clean and very much squeezed. Do a test rushed to focus solace level. Too short or too tight may bring about you - or others - to be diverted or uncomfortable. Minimize adornments. Keep in mind: toning it down would be best. You need to be critical for the right reasons.

Know the location of your interview. Do a drive-by if possible. Plan to arrive at the designated office 10 minutes in advance. Do not forget to bring extra copies of your resume in a folder or portfolio. Bring a small notebook for notes, but keep note-taking to a minimum.

Gather business cards from each person with whom you meet. Approach about time allotments for filling the position, how and when you will be advised, and on the off chance that they would like extra data or materials from you. Try not to ASK ABOUT SALARY OR BENEFITS!

Follow Up: Send a card to say thanks inside of 24-48 hours of your meeting. Send one to each individual who talked to you. E-mail is OK. However, talk for formal business correspondence, which is constantly more formal than commonplace e-mail. Utilize the card to say thanks to repeat your advantage and to stress your particular capabilities for the position. What do you need them to recollect about you that is prone to "offer" them on you as a feasible competitor? Everything about the pursuit of employment ought to be centered on what YOU can accomplish for the organization, what YOU convey to the position, and why the head honcho ought to contract YOU! The meeting may be your one shot - so make it a decent one!

Chapter 9: Staying Calm During The Interview

Now, the day of the interview finally came. You have gone a long way already and you have no reason to mess it up. Just stay calm and stick to the belief that things will turn out fine. In order for you to truly stay calm during your session, here are some useful tricks and techniques that will assist you in getting through the experience with flying colors:

Give yourself sufficient relaxation time, so you need to arrive really early. As mentioned earlier, it is always best to be there ten to fifteen minutes before the scheduled interview. That way, you have enough time to "get the feel" of the environment. Sit down, relax, and compose yourself. Breathe in and breathe out so that you can gather the thoughts that you need and eliminate the unnecessary jitters. If you are a bit nervous, just remember that it is not only the company that checks you out; you are also checking out the company. Maintaining that mantra will help you maintain your calmness and confidence.

Assume that this is just a normal yet professional conversation. Again, you are not the only one who is being put to test here. By looking at it as a conversation, you will be more open and more confident to answer the questions being thrown at you. Flash that smile of confidence and it will make a big difference. Be at ease, it is okay to open up and share what you think.

Gather your confidence and positivity. Before the interview, visualize that "perfect ten" performance. Imagine yourself responding to all questions confidently and impressively. Of course, in the actual interview, you might find yourself with shaking hands or unstable voice. In such moments, just remember that it is okay to stop for a few seconds, take a few deep breaths and proceed with renewed calm. Remember, you are invited to do the interview because someone saw your CV and he thinks that you might do well. That alone is enough reason to celebrate, because someone knew that you have what it takes. So, you should not be nervous. You will do well if you choose to do well. You can do great if you choose to do great.

The interviewer is not a prosecutor. Look at him as a friend. If you will see him as a foe, then you are definitely in trouble. You will have the hostile tendency and you might not be able to respond to his questions in the most logical manner possible. If you want to be treated pleasantly, give your interviewer sufficient reason to treat you as such. He is not a machine created to reject unworthy applicants. Rather, he is also a human being doing his job.

Do not fiddle around. Just sit up steady and straight. Try to maintain this formal stance throughout the interview because it helps in maintaining your confidence and in the projection of your voice. Proper posture helps you exude confidence even if you are really trembling.

Never show that you are stressed by the interview situation. Show that you are capable of being graceful despite the pressure. This way, your interviewer will see you as a person who can take on any challenge. And that's a big plus.

Focus on your personal purpose and back it up with your inherent strengths. Do not be anxious because it will make you feel that your purpose may not measure up or your strengths might not be worthy of comparison. At any point during the interview, do not panic. With the clear purpose in mind backed up by your professional skills, you will be able to get through the interview successfully.

Take your time and normalize your breathing. Remember, you do not have to answer the question the moment the interviewer finishes his question. You can respond after 5 to 10 seconds and that is more than enough to gather your thoughts and formulate your response. Take a deep breath because it drives more oxygen into your bloodstream. The oxygen can help you feel more relaxed.

Do not pretend that you are perfect. Never be disappointed if at any point, you commit a mistake. Remember, employers know for a fact that there exist no perfect employees, so you do not really have to be one. Admit instances when you made mistakes in the past. That will create a very good impression because it shows that you have the sense of responsibility and accountability.

Finally, you need to think of this: the interview that you are having is just one of your many options. There are many other jobs that are available out there. Do not pressure yourself that much to the point of breaking. By adopting this kind of thinking, you will maintain a calm stance and you will not worry that much. Constantly remind yourself that there are other jobs waiting for you out there.

Chapter 10: What Are Your Greatest Strengths?

One of the most simple interview questions is, "what are your strengths?" Most employers these days will not ask this question in a straightforward manner. It will sometimes be phrased as, "what qualities you have that you feel are important?" or something along those lines. However, there are still companies out there that will flat out ask you this question, and it helps to be prepared for it.

What the Interviewer is looking for?

In asking this question, the interviewer wants to know specifically how your skills, traits, and experiences match up with the job you're interviewing for.

How to not answer the question?

A common mistake when answering this question is to give the interviewer strengths that do not correspond to the requirements of the job you're interviewing for. For example, if you're applying for a sales job, you don't want to describe your computer skills. Computer skills may be a valuable strength, but they probably don't have much to do with doing sales, unless you would be selling from a website.

How to Answer the Question

In order to answer this question efficiently, it is a good idea to take the time to write down your greatest strengths. When writing down your strengths, you should divide them into three categories:

☐ Personal Traits – Think about the strongest personal qualities you have and how they can contribute to success on the job (i.e. being strategic, flexible, creative, dependable, punctual, analytical, or a team player). All these traits are ideal, but it is important that you highlight two or three key traits that will contribute to success on the job.

☐ Knowledge-based Skills – These are skills that you have obtained from previous work experiences, internships and educational experiences. (I.e. field of specialty, technical skills, and languages).

☐ Transferable Skills – Skills that can be transferable from a previous job or social organization involvement (i.e., communication skills, people skills, leadership skills, and problem solving skills).

After you write these down, review the job description and see which of your skills matches the qualifications of the job. For the best answer, take one skill from each category and formulate an answer that will impress the interviewer.

Sample **Answer**

Q. Tell me about your greatest strengths

A. I personally pride myself on my ability to _____, _____ and _____. I understand this job requires someone who has these skills.

I've personally developed these skills through my internship/leadership experience at _____ and I know that this position requires someone who has great _____ and _____ skills. The fact that I do possess these skills will allow me to be successful in this position and fit in with your company.

This is a straight answer that quickly gets to the point. As you can see, I've listed three important skills/traits it takes to be successful in this job. I also explained to the interviewer where I learned these skills and how the company will benefit from them.

Chapter 11: The Typical Interview: An Introduction To The Process

The process of securing and performing well in a job interview can be challenging, but it is ultimately one of the most rewarding endeavors on which you can embark: securing your ideal job is one way in which to gain entry into whatever elite group you've always wanted to be a part of. While there is no truly typical job interview—the experience encompasses too many variables (candidate, employer, field, and so on) to be wholly predictable—there are some common elements that occur in most interview situations. Understanding the basics of interviewer's categories of questions, as well as honing your ability to answer clearly and cleverly, can give you a significant advantage in the interview process. The importance of a job interview really cannot be overstated: this simple act is the culmination of your years of hard work, focus, and energy. You may have paid tens of thousands of dollars for a higher education or special training just to get to this point; you may have spent your entire life dreaming of this particular job in this particular field; you may have an inkling that this job might be able to propel you to success and security in ways you have heretofore only dreamed of.

Job interviews are complex enterprises, as well. You are selling yourself, of course—your set of skills, your personality, your professionalism—but you are also hoping to present your ability to be part of a larger team or company. Indeed, part of the process of interviewing requires understanding subtle and psychological cues; you are not the only person involved, of course, and you need to be able to "read the room," as it were. While there are no specific set of rules for any given situation, as each situation will be markedly different, there are some general ideas about how you can prepare yourself for any eventuality that you might happen upon in an interview. This is what this guide is for, to help you review the heart of the interview process, the kinds of questions you will likely be asked, along with how you might best answer them using particularly tested techniques.

Attending a job interview is a potentially life-changing event, so it should be approached with great deliberation and care—as well as the knowledge that the interview is far more important to you than it is to the interviewer. Having been made aware of that, however, it also behooves you to know something about the interviewer—when possible—and certainly to do research on the company itself. Armed with more information always makes you appear to be a better candidate, well-informed, and eager to join this new group.

Thinking about what kinds of questions the interviewer may ask, and preparing some possible answers to potential questions is some of the most valuable research you can conduct. Certainly, you cannot predict every question the interviewer will ask, but you can anticipate some basic ones, based on the job requirements, your own resume, and the knowledge of standard questions frequently asked.

Be sure to review your resume and cover letter before the interview (and, by all means, do bring these with you for reference, of course). It is likely that the interviewer will ask you specific questions related to one or more of your past experiences. The better you know your own resume, the stronger a candidate you will seem. Also think about specific experiences in past working relationships that you might mention or highlight in the interview; the resume lists your experience and your accomplishments, but it doesn't give a clear sense of how you interact with superiors or colleagues in a working situation, and it would be prudent of you to have some stories prepared detailing some of those experiences. Listing your skill set, including both hard and soft skills, will help you to highlight what it is about your professional and/or educational experience that sets you apart from other candidates.

You should also be very clear on what the duties and expectations of the position that you are applying for are: what, specifically, does the job require and how best will you be able to fulfill those expectations? A job advertisement will sometimes give you just a few lines of explanation; at other times, it will have a lengthy description. Either way, make it your responsibility, prior to the interview, to find out all you can about the position itself so that you can directly address how your past experiences and present skills can best be suited for said position.

Beyond the position itself, it is always important to understand the broader working culture of the company as a whole. This ensures that you can demonstrate that you are a good fit, not only for the specific job but for the company in general. This includes understanding whether the work environment is collaborative or highly individualized; this difference alone will determine how you will respond to questions asked by the interviewer, as well as whether you are, ultimately, a good fit. Obviously, when you study the company, look into its working practices and traditions. Notice, as well, when you submit your resume or attend your interview, how employees appear to interact and work. This kind of observation can give you a sense of job satisfaction and collegiality in any workplace. It can certainly give you the information needed to make a final decision about which job to take, assuming that you have more than one offer or the resources to make your decision only when you are certain that you are a good fit.

In addition to knowing yourself, your interviewer, the job requirements, and company culture, you should also be prepared to ask or ascertain the potential for growth that is inherent to the position. That is, understanding what is required of the specific position is crucial, but knowing what opportunities might exist beyond it is also a way to impress your interviewer that you have even more to offer. In addition, this information is crucial to your personal decision-making process: depending on your age at the time of the interview, it may be very important that you move beyond whatever position you are applying for at the current time. Indicating that you are prepared to learn more or to take on more at the very beginning gives the impression that you are eager to integrate into the company from the start.

Certainly, it is also the case that you should be prepared to ask about salary and benefits if such things were not made abundantly clear before the interview. This kind of information is obviously important for your own decision-making process, but it is also crucial that you make clear your expectations from the start, as well. When asking about salary and benefits, already have prepared what you will be satisfied to take; that is, don't ask the question without having your own answer ready, as many interviewers will respond by asking you what your expectations are.

Finally, the importance of attitude cannot be overstated: in the end, if you are enthusiastic, prepared, and knowledgeable, this will go a long way towards presenting yourself as an ideal employee. Throughout this guide, you will gain tips on what to do before the interview—building a resume, creating a cover letter, researching the company, outlining your story, and reducing stress—as well as how to develop particular interview skills that will give you that winning approach to interviews for success every time.

Chapter 12: What To Include

There are several things you will want to include on your resume. You should include any skill or talent that could potentially apply to the position you are seeking. These can be skills you acquired during your education or work experience. You can even include skills that you have acquired during life experience that are applicable to the position you are seeking.

You should include your college education on your resume. Include any colleges that you attended, even if you did not graduate from them. If you did not graduate, mention your area of study and any accomplishments during your term there. If you are currently enrolled, include your expected date of graduation, expected degree, accomplishments, and perhaps a brief list of courses that have prepared you for the position.

For work experience you should include any jobs that you have held within the last five years or more. If you have only a few positions under your belt you can list them all. If you have many positions over a long period of time, only include those positions that relate to the current position you are seeking. If all of them relate, include only the last five years of work history. You do not want to fill many pages with work history that will never be read by the potential employer.

Do not worry about gaps in work history. You can answer any questions about these gaps when asked, which may come up in the interview process. Make sure you are ready to answer these questions. If you have work history in your current career field interrupted by work history in another industry, you can feel free to leave out the other industry experience on your resume. When asked about the gap in employment dates you can explain that you had a position that does not relate to the one you are seeking.

What To Leave Out

Do not put your high school or grade school education on your resume. Only college education belongs on a professional resume. It is generally assumed that you have a high school diploma or GED for most positions.

Do not include skills or talents that do not relate to the position you are seeking. Do not include hobbies or any other information about your personal life on the resume. Your resume should only include information about your professional life and experiences.

If you have gaps in employment you should not try to explain these in your resume. Save this information for your interview, and only volunteer it if asked about it. Many homemakers tend to put something on their resume to that effect. A common entry on these resumes is "domestic engineer." This is actually very unprofessional and should be omitted. If asked about your long gap in work history you can explain that you have been a homemaker for the last however many years, and are now ready to reenter the workforce.

Do not include side jobs that are irrelevant to the position you are seeking. If, for example, you worked as a waitress in a restaurant while paying your way through college, you probably shouldn't include that on a professional resume. The exception is that if this is the only work experience you have as a recent college graduate, you can include that short entry on the work history section of your functional resume.

Finally, do not include references on your resume. References clutter up a resume and make it longer than necessary. You can create a separate page for references if you like. In truth, few employers call and verify references. Many employers don't even ask for them anymore. If an employer wants references they will request them. Do not include them on your resume.

A Word about Formatting

You want your resume to both be professional and stand out. When trying to make your resume stand out from the rest, it is tempting to use a lot of fancy fonts and styles. This is actually a huge mistake.

Using fancy fonts or large type can actually detract from your resume. It might catch the eye of whoever is sorting the mail, but it might also cause them to think that you are unprofessional, leading to them passing over your resume for those of other candidates.

Use a simple, italicized font in a slightly larger type for your name, then use a normal font for the rest of your resume. You might break up your resume with clear lines between the sections. You might put in a page boarder to give it a framed look. These are fine, and can make your resume stand out while still giving it a professional appearance.

Sample Chronological Resume

Your Name

Your address
Your Phone number
Your email address

Objective: To locate a position within a company that will advance my skills and knowledge in this industry and help me further my career through opportunities for advancement.

Education: Bachelor of Science, Information Technology University of Michigan
Graduated with honors, January 1984

Skills: Graphic design Microsoft Office Publisher
Computer software Computer hardware Customer support
Typing 90 wpm Correspondence Basic clerical

Work History: IT Support Technician Company, Inc. June 2004-Present
Duties: List several duties here that you performed in this position. Try to focus on

duties and tasks that relate to the position you are seeking. Keep it as brief and concise as possible.

Accomplishments: Include any accomplishments that truly show your superiority in your career field that relate to the position you are seeking. This is entirely optional.

IT Help Desk Representative Company, Inc. Jan 1990-June 2004 Duties: Again, list all applicable duties you performed.

IT Intern Company, Inc. Jan 1984-Dec 1984 Duties: List duties you performed. Skills Acquired: If you had an internship or fellowship position during or after college you should include a bit about what you learned from that experience.Sample Functional Resume

Your Name

Your address
Your phone number
Your email address

Objective: To gain experience in my chosen career field while building on my skills and education.

Education: Bachelor of Science, Business Administration University of Missouri Focus on Human Resources Management Expected graduation Aug 2015

Skills/Abilities: Microsoft Office Basic clerical Payroll OSHA administration DOT administration HPPA regulations Employee Training Employee Evaluation Best hiring practices HR software Withholding administration Policy administration Evaluating applications Applicant interviews Database management (List as many skills, abilities and talents as you can in this section. The more the better.)

Accomplished: List here things you accomplished during your schooling or internships. Include any recognitions for hard work, performance or academics.

Work History: HR Intern Company, Inc. Jan 2015-June 2015

Shift Leader IHOP Aug 2013-Jan 2015

Server Waffle House Aug 2012-July 2013

Questions to Ask Your Interviewers

It is a guarantee that your interviewer will ask you if you have any questions. It is a bad idea to leave this open. You should have at least a few questions for your interviewer. This will show that you have given the position and the company some thought.

Depending on information in the job posting and information provided by the interviewer, you might want to ask questions about the position itself. If it is not clear what role the position plays in the company, feel free to ask those questions. Beware, however, of looking too ignorant of the way these duties relate to the company as a whole. That can hurt your chances of being chosen for the position.

There are some standard questions you can have ready for any interview. For example, you can ask what the culture of the company is like. You can ask what a typical day at the office might hold. You might also ask questions such as what software programs or equipment the company uses, then demonstrate your knowledge of said systems.

Your questions should lead to brief exchanges of information or ideas. They should not be simple question and answer. This way you will be able to continue the conversational mood of the interview that you have hopefully already established.

You should have researched the company before the interview. However, if you were unable to find much information about the company online, you might have some questions about the company itself. You might ask if they do global or national business, what kind of clientele they have, or what their mission statement is.

Never ask the interviewer questions about benefits or salary. You should avoid these questions and save them for when you are offered a position. When you ask about benefits and salary you are telling the interviewer that you are only interested in what you can get from the job. This makes them think you are not interested in the position itself, which can hurt your chances of being hired for the position.

Finally, ask the interviewer about the next step in the hiring process. By doing so you are showing that you are still very interested in the position. This is the equivalent of asking for another interview or for the job itself. It also shows confidence. It will give you information about what to expect to happen next. You should also ask when you might hear from them.

Few Final Tips and Not "Tricks"

You should never try to trick your way into an interview or a job. You will only fail once you get into the position. Anyone who claims to have tricks for getting through an interview is not being honest about how interviews work. In fact, they are telling you to be dishonest in your hiring process, which is the worst thing you can do.

There are three important tips that cannot be stressed enough.

Be yourself.

You should not try to be someone you are not. It will only serve to make you more nervous and uncomfortable, and the interview will not go well. While you do not want to talk to the interviewer as you would a friend or family member, you do want to let your own personality come through in your conversation.

Be honest.

Your answers to the interviewer's questions will come much easier if you are completely honest. When you draw on real experiences to answer questions you will be more comfortable and your answers will come more easily. This will show through to the interviewer and they will see that you are being honest with them. Interviewers are trained to tell when someone is lying, and if they suspect that you are making stuff up they will end the interview quickly.

Be confident.

When you are confident in your ability to perform the job you are interviewing for, you will be more likely to land that job. Your confidence will shine through in your conversation and your body language. The interviewer will see that you are able to handle any situation, and that you are comfortable with your level of knowledge and abilities.

The Final Day

The night before your interview you should get a good night's sleep. Make sure you are well rested before your interview. You do not want to appear tired at all. Tiredness can be easily misinterpreted as boredom or a lack of preparation.

The morning of your interview leave yourself at least two hours to prepare before leaving the house. You should shower, shave, style your hair, choose just the right clothing, and dress carefully. You should examine your choice of jewelry and make sure that your appearance is entirely professional.

Once you are physically ready for your interview, make yourself mentally ready. Practice your answers to questions you expect to hear in your interview. Practice them in front of the mirror. This will get your mind working and awake so that you are prepared to carry on a good conversation with your interviewer.

Give yourself plenty of time to get to your interview. Plan for poor traffic or other delays. If your commute is expected to take 30 minutes, give yourself 45 minutes for travel time. You can always wait in your car if you get there too early.

Go into the interview 10-15 minutes early. You do not want to go in earlier than that, or it will appear that you are not organized. If you go in just before the interview time it will appear that you run late or just barely on time. If you were working there you would show up for work 10-15 minutes early to have time to put your stuff away and be at your station ready to work when your shift started. You should always assume the attitude that you have the position when you go in for the interview, so 10-15 minutes early is a good guideline.

If you are seated to wait for the interviewer, stand up as they approach. Shake their hand and introduce yourself, and tell them you are glad to be there. Follow them into the interview room and sit down quietly. You can wait for them to begin, or you can start off with some small talk to ease into the conversation.

Remember your practiced answers to the interview questions. Practice good listening skills. Treat the interview as a friendly conversation rather than a formal question and answer session. This will help you stay more relaxed and able to meet the demands of anything that arises in the interview.

At the end of the interview, shake their hand and thank them for their time. Let them know you look forward to hearing from them soon. This tells them that you are still interested in the job and that you are expecting an answer in the positive.

Following Up

You should always follow up after an interview. Do not just leave it up to the employer to contact you when they make a decision. Following up is especially important if you are one of the first candidates to be interviewed. You want to remind the employer that you are a valid candidate, and the best for the job.

Follow up the same day of your interview with a simple email thanking the interviewer for their time. Tell them how much you enjoyed your conversation, and how you look forward to speaking with them again soon.

Four to five business days later you should follow up again with a phone call to the interviewer. Tell them again how much you enjoyed your conversation, and ask how the hiring process is progressing. Offer to come in again to discuss the position, and make it clear (without being demanding) that you are very interested in the position.

If you have not heard anything within two or three days after your follow up phone call, send another email asking about the status of your hiring process. At this point you may be considered the prime candidate but for whatever reason they are not ready to hire. Another possibility is that you may have been declined for the position and the company did not notify you. Either way it is important for you to know whether or not to continue your efforts in trying to gain a position with the employer, or if you should look elsewhere for employment.

Chapter 13: Making Sure To Have The Right Mindset For Interview

1. Persistence is Key

You cannot expect to achieve success overnight in business. You may ask a person to vouch for you that you know that works in the company. This is not to say that you will use the connection to move right to being hired, but at least it will let the company know that you would be a good addition to their organization.

2. The process of the interview is two-way

Yes it is normal to let the recruiter lead the process, but you should also prepare to interview him/her. This is perfectly natural after all you are going to be in the company if you are accepted so the hiring manager will not be offended. Just picture the interview with just them asking you questions, and you putting or adding nothing to the conversation other than answering their questions. It may seem like you are just trying to get the interview over with as soon as possible.

3. Be part of the company even when you are still in the application process

Before you have your interview make a list of things that you can do, beside each item mark those that are needed by this particular company. Read them and memorize them. If there is other requirements that you cannot at this point provide them with start learning them and finding out more about them.

When the recruiter asks you "what can you contribute to the company?" You will know your answers because you took the time to memorize them. If the topic goes towards the things that you are not trained in yet you will at least have a basic knowledge about them. This will show the recruiter that you are eager to learn about them and expand your knowledge.

4. References Make a Big Difference

When you are submitting a resume make sure that you have the proper people listed as your references. You should gauge your references according to the position that you are applying for. Make sure that you warn people ahead of time that you have used their name as a reference. Make sure that the people that you choose are in good terms with you.

5. You need to practice, practice!

There is nothing wrong with practicing for your interview. You can easily do this alone by facing a mirror and rehearse the answers that you are planning on giving your interviewer. Watch to make sure that you are using proper posture and are speaking clearly. Ask a friend or family member to pretend to be the recruiting manager and let them lead the interview.

Chapter 14: What Is Your Maximum Value?

Understanding what your maximum value is will help you decide what positions you should apply for, the regions and locations, as well as what companies. Websites such as Glassdoor.com can help you compare your position through different companies and see the average pay scale. It allows you to compare and contrast the same position for the companies you apply for and from there you will be able to choose the higher paying positions for your qualifications.

Furthermore, websites like this can aid you in knowing if the company in question is one which will allow you longevity. Employees past and present are able to comment and rate the company giving you a better insight into how the company is run and if you should be consider other positions due to factors which may not fit with your lifestyle. For instance, if you do not want a position which requires you to travel and you see travel is extensive for your position at a certain company, then you quickly know that position may not be the best fit.

In contrast this website will also allow you the capability of knowing what perks the company has to offer. Perhaps they have a 401k match program which other companies do not, or perhaps they have tuition payback. Glassdoor.com gives wonderful insights into a company and its inner workings without having to dig too deeply. Do take every comment from past and present employees with a grain of salt however. Disgruntled employees are often unkind towards their employers regardless if the company is wonderful to work for or not and every person will have a different experience with an employer. One person may not get along with the manager and another works perfectly. It is always best to remain objective.

Another site which is helpful in comparing and contrasting is smartasset.com which has a cost of living calculator. If you are applying for positions all over the world or country, utilizing their cost of living tool with the average salary function on Glassdoor.com will give you a better insight of what positions are really most lucrative. One state may have a lower cost of living and therefore a lower salary range but you may find the salary remains the same across the board in which case, if you are able and capable of moving, you will have a larger income in a location with a lower cost of living.

In the case of understanding your maximum value it is important to avoid believing you will get the top salary if you are just starting your career. It is important to be realistic in what you bring to the table. If you have many credentials you can certainly push towards the top salary but knowing the economic climate for the region in which you are applying will give you better insight as to what your true salary will most likely be.

Also important to avoid is taking everything you find on a web page as gospel. Again, any comments made my past or present employees should be understood as only the perspective of that person and not necessarily the overall feel from everyone at the company. If you chose to apply and obtain an interview looking at the climate while at the location is a more true glimpse into the world of that company.

Furthermore, if considering relocation, checking with real estate agents in the location for which you may be moving, will give you a clearer idea of what the cost of living and economic climate is like. Perhaps rent is cheap but food is expensive. Maybe there is a location within commuting distance which will allow you to maximize your income without difficulty.

Chapter 15: Preparing For Phone Interview

Many job interviews today require a phone interview first before going to the face to face stage of the interview process. This is a good and practical system. The interviewer will be able to know right away if the applicant is going to be a good fit for the job they are offering. Your tone of voice will dictate your confidence level. If the recruiter senses a lack of confidence in the voice of the applicant it is highly unlikely that they will be called back for this position. Below are some tips for you on how you can ace a phone interview:

1. Think of Phone interview as a Personal Interview

Most companies will do up to several sets of interviews—whether you pass the phone interview or not you will still have face to face interviews to do. This is a good setup because you are given the chance to redeem yourself at the face to face interview. If the company you are applying to wants to do a step by step process meaning that you must pass the first step to move on to the next one. So if you fail the phone interview that will be the end of the road for you with some companies. So it is important that you remember to treat the phone interview like it is a personal interview.

2. Being Comfortable During Phone Interview

Make sure to be wearing an outfit that makes you feel comfortable and good to wear. This will make you feel and sound more positive during your phone interview. If you are feeling good it will come out in the tone of your voice.

3. Location

Having phone interviews is not unusual in today's world. Often a recruiter will call and ask if it is a good time to have interview with you or would you like to do it at a set time. Calmly say to the recruiter a good time that would work better for you to have the interview then set it up. Make sure that you choose a location that is going to be calm and quiet. Alert your family members when you will be having your interview and ask them to keep quiet during this time.

4. Never Reveal what your Salary Expectation is

You should never reveal your salary expectation during a phone interview. This is just a way for the recruiter to put you on the spot. Calmly state that if everything goes well in the personal interview that salary will not matter. If they press you just explain to them that you are not comfortable discussing numbers before you have had a chance to see the environment of the company, and how the employees work there.

5. Avoid using Idiot board

A common mistake during a phone interview is laying out all your notes in front of you, it will only distract you from answering the questions the phone interviewer is asking you. Instead just concentrate on what the recruiter is asking you.

Chapter 16: What Is A Job Interview Anyway?

After sending your application letter and waiting for around ten days, if you're lucky enough, you will be invited to attend a recruitment test. The company will usually contact you via email or telephone, so don't forget to include these details in your application letter and resume or CV.

RECRUITMENT TEST

The number of applicants invited to a recruitment test varies depending on the number of new employees the company needs.

In general, the recruitment test consists of three stages:
1) Psychological test,
2) Skills test,
3) Interview.

These tests usually adopt a pass/fail grading system. This means that only few candidates will make it to the interview stage.

INTERVIEW

Compared with any other tests, the interview is the most crucial part of the hiring process. This ultimate test will determine your success or failure in the entire job search process.

Therefore, make sure that you are well prepared for the interview. Remember, this test is much more important than any other test in your life. Your whole future will be determined here.

Many job seekers see the interview as the most daunting and terrifying test. It's because during an interview you are completely on your own. You cannot depend on anyone but yourself. You have to demonstrate your ability, think fast and respond logically in a short space of time.

Like any other test, the key to a successful interview is to practice over and over again. The interview is the final stage of the recruitment process. After choosing the right job, searching for job opportunities, sending application letters, completing psychological and skill tests, you have finally arrived at the final door which will determine whether or not you will join the workforce. Now is the most important and decisive moment in your life! This is your chance to build a better future. The opportunity is there so you have to put all your effort into it.

There are many kinds of interview test, and the most popular ones are one-on-one, panel, and group interviews. Regardless of the format, you have to demonstrate your skills and capabilities here. You have to convince the company that you are the best candidate to fill the position. Not only on paper but in real life. This is the real fight!

TWO-WAY PROCESS

The one thing job seekers frequently forget during an interview is that is a two-way, not one-way, process. The company invites you along to a recruitment test because they are interested in your skills and background.

If you are able to prove your capabilities, it won't only be you who wants to land the job; the company will want you to fill the position! I have experienced this time and again.

EVALUATION CRITERIA

Companies evaluate three key areas:

1) Skills/Intelligence = 50%
2) Experience = 25%
3) Personality = 25%

Skills and intelligence play a crucial role in the recruitment process because all companies want smart and reliable employees. Their benchmarks include school and college grades, and your score in the skills test.

The second component is experience. Most companies prefer more experienced candidates because they won't have to waste time and money training and educating new employees. An experienced candidate has a better understanding of his/her duties enabling them to quickly adapt to their role.

Nevertheless, there are situations in which a company prefers inexperienced candidates or fresh graduates, for example:

1) If there are no experienced candidates applying for the job;

2) The job in question is an entry-level position reserved for fresh graduates and the company has enough time to train and educate new employees.

Therefore, if you read a job advertisement that looks for experienced candidates, don't be discouraged. As long as you're confident that you can do the job, just do apply!

The last aspect that will be evaluated by the company is the personality or attitude of the candidates. These include their honesty, diligence, integrity, etc.

All of these will be measured during the psychological test and interview, which will ultimately determine whether a candidate passes or fails the recruitment test.

A candidate may have a great set of skills and knowledge, but if their personality is not in line with the company's vision and mission, their chances of getting the job would be low.

COMMON MISTAKES

One common mistake young job seekers make is not preparing for the test. It's ironic that the same people who are willing to spend hours and even stay up all night before a school exam to study are the same people who don't study, or worse still, do nothing at all before a much more important test. A test that will determine their future happiness!

The reason for this is simple. First, they don't know the test material. Second, they don't know what to study!

Chapter 17: Questions On Salary, Promotion And Benefits

How much was your last salary?

Most times, this question is hardly asked during job interviews. However, it is exclusively for people whose curriculum vitae show that they have been working. This is why this question is not asked to job seekers whose application packages show that they are fresh or new in the labor market. If the above question is asked, it is expected that the job you applied for should have higher and better prospects than the past ones. This means that the salary of the prospective job should be higher than your past salaries. If the difference is too wide, you may be considered under qualified for the job. You will be considered overqualified for the job if the salary of your past job is also higher than that of the job you applied for. But the exact difference, most likely, will be unknown to you since you know of the past salary alone. If you had/have a job with a good salary, mention the amount. Do not exaggerate or inflate your past salary because you may not have sufficient evidence, especially bank documents, to defend your false claim, if it is requested. Besides, some employers confirm their applicants' claims on salary prior to making a job offer. However, if your last salary is far below your salary expectation from the prospective job, politely appeal to the interviewer to wave the question aside.

Sample Answers

I am a fresh graduate. So, I have not been on salary as an employee.

I will crave your indulgence to wave this question aside because I am more concerned about the future than the past.

About how much do you expect to be paid as salary?

Try as much as you can to find the salary the organization is will be willing to pay if you are offered an appointment. Your ability to achieve this will help you not to overprice or underprice when you are asked this question. If, however, you were unable to find the salary structure of the organization and the amount the organization will be willing to pay if you are offered the appointment, you should apply caution in answering this question. The first caution to apply is to avoid mentioning anything about compensation or remuneration, before the question is asked. If salary-related issue should arise, let it be raised by the interviewer. Do not be in a haste in responding to this question. You should not give a specific answer to this question because the amount you mention may be too high or too low. In other words, you may overprice or underprice. You may not be considered for the job if the amount you mention is too high, as the employer may be afraid that you cannot be at home with the organization with the amount it can afford to pay. You may also be rejected on the ground that your standard is below that of the company, if the amount you mention is too low. One of the best approaches to answering this question is to give an open and unspecific answer. Another approach is to tell the interviewer that you have insufficient information to estimate your salary. If, however, you belong to a professional body that has a standard for the remuneration of different categories of its members, you can cite their recommendation/standard. The sample answers below reflect these categories of answers.

Sample Answers

I believe the salaries of your employees are determined by your corporate policy, and accepting your policy is a requisite for being an employee of your organization.

All other things equal, I know that the salary of an employee is determined by a variety of factors. This includes the value/worth of the employee, the status of the organization and the responsibilities and challenges of the job. I do not have enough information to comment on the salary, as I know of the first factor only - my value.

I am a member of the Institute of Chartered Accountants. The institute specifies that members who have my qualifications should be paid a minimum of Nabc,000 per annum. I expect that my salary should be within that range.

Is salary among the factors that determine the satisfaction you derive from a job?

Sample Answer

Though my salary has a role to play in making me happy in a job, it is not the most important thing to me about work. I am more interested in the career prospects of the job and its impact on my personal development.

How often do you expect increase in your salary?

Sample Answer

I believe this would be determined by a number of factors. This includes the policy of the company, my productivity in the organization and the overall success of the company.

How would you justify your salary?

Sample Answer

I expect to be paid from the money I make for the company, and I know that the organization will remain in existence only when the employees generate more money than they are paid. I will justify my income by ensuring that my services to the company surpass my remuneration.

What are your expectations if you are hired?

This question is not as simple as it appears to be. Just as you (should) have some expectations from the job you applied for and your prospective employer, the organization also has its expectations from you. However, you should choose a job because of your expectations from it but justify your interest in the job by emphasising the interest and expectations of the prospective employer. The expectations organizations are delighted with are employees' contributions to their success. Hence, do not say, "I expect the company to be prompt in the payment of salary". Also do not say, "I hope the company will soon increase my salary". You should also avoid saying, "I expect to be promoted very soon". Also avoid saying, "I hope the company will sponsor my vacations". No organization will offer you an appointment because of your expectations from it. Every prospective employer's interest in a job seeker is determined by its expectations - the value the job seeker will add to its organization. This is the area your answer should focus.

Sample Answers

I expect to be an invaluable asset to your organization if I am offered an appointment.

I hope to assist the company to the best of my ability in achieving her organizational goals.

If the interviewer insists on knowing your expectations from the job which will profit you, you should tell him about what you hope to profit from the job if you get the appointment. The expectation should have long term significance. Such question may be, **"Do you have other expectations from this job?"**

Sample Answer

I hope this job will afford me the opportunity to advance my career, if I get the appointment.

How soon do you hope to be promoted?

Sample Answer

I believe that my promotion will be determined by the policy of the company. I also know that my performance also has a role to play in earning my promotion because I will not be qualified for promotion until I am overqualified for the position I occupy.

Has your salary been delayed before?

Sample Answer

My past employers were very prompt in payment.

Has your salary ever been reduced?

Sample Answer

I am yet to have that experience in a place of work.

What would you do if your salary is delayed for any reason?

Sample Answer

It depends on the factor that is responsible for the delay. As an accountant, I will always know when the company is making profit and when it is having financial challenges. I am confident that the organization cannot afford to risk her reputation by owing the employees at a time it is making profit, and I also know that this organization has a reputation for accelerated growth.

Will you leave us if you get a better offer?

"**How soon would you join us if you are employed?**" Both questions are related, likewise their answers. Your answers to both questions should cohere. In the book, it was advised that you should be very careful with your answer because the prospective employer will not expect you to (promise to) start the new job immediately if you claimed to be working with an organization. It was also remarked that it is wrong to resign from a job without prior notification in order to join a new organization. In addition, it was noted that the interviewer may be afraid that you are not saying the truth or that you will frustrate their organizational activities with an abrupt resignation if you get a better job while with them, if you promise to start immediately. While answering the question, "**Will you leave us if you get a better offer?**", do not be in a haste with denying that you will not accept a better offer if it comes your way in the future. Remember, you aspire for progress, and one of the ways of achieving that is getting a job that is better than the one you applied for, even if you are offered appointment. You should be mindful of the fact that the interviewer is not ignorant of this. Consequently, exercise diplomacy and caution in answering this question.

Sample Answer

I desire progress in life. I also desire to advance my career. I know that I may not achieve that without getting a better job. However, I do not consider a job as a better one just because it has a higher remuneration. There are other conditions like job security and future prospects which are more important to me. However, I will not be in a haste to leave your organization so that I will not frustrate your activities. Since I will likely not spend the rest of my working years in your organization, I will respect your policy whenever I am about to resign.

Chapter 18: Your Resume

Why can I not get an Interview?

I have a simple rule:

If you are sending your resume off to lots of job applications but NOT being called up for any interviews; there is something wrong with your resume.

If you ARE being called up for interviews but not getting the job, the problem is NOT with your resume but with your interview technique.

In this chapter we will discuss the first scenario – you have sent your resume off scores of times but are not being asked to attend any interviews.

The fact that lots of different people have seen your resume but decided NOT to select you for an interview is NOT a coincidence. There is something wrong with your resume.

If you are currently in this position, my advice to you is to STOP sending your resume out immediately until you have brought it up to scratch:

Albert Einstein defined 'insanity' as:

"doing the same thing over and over again and expecting different results."

It is insane to keep sending the same resume out again and again and expecting a different result. You won't get a different result until you send a different one.

Have a good read of it. Be honest - if you were an employer and you received this resume would you want to interview the candidate?

Below are some useful tips for you to consider that will help you change it from a "we will keep you on file" resume to a "we would very much like to interview you!" resume.

Resume Tip 1: Check your spelling and grammar

The very first thing to check on your resume is your spelling and grammar.

Companies can sometimes receive hundreds of resumes when a job is advertised. They have neither the time nor the inclination to read them all and bad spelling and grammar is a sure fire way to ensure that yours goes straight in the bin.

All word processors have a spellcheck feature – has your resume been spell checked?

If English language, spelling and grammar is not your strength, ask somebody else to have a look at it as discussed below.

Resume Tip 2: Get somebody to review your Resume

A few years ago my sister-in-law was desperate to become a primary school teacher but despite having all the required teaching qualifications and applying for many jobs, she couldn't even get an interview.

Eventually she asked a friend of the family who happened to be a very experienced teacher, to have a look at the resume to see if he could shed any light on the lack of interest.

The kindly teacher responded by admitting that if his school had received her resume they would have thrown it straight in the bin. This came as a shock to my sister-in-law as she didn't think there was anything wrong with it.

However, she took his advice on board and modified her resume as per his recommendations and I am delighted to say that she is now a very happy and popular primary school teacher.

The lesson to learn from this story is that YOU may think your resume is fine but your potential employer may NOT!

Don't be ashamed to ask people for help – pride will NOT get you a job. The more people who can look at the resume and give you tips the better.

Do you know anybody who is involved in recruitment who looks at resumes every day? If so ask them to look at yours.

There are also may agencies and professionals who will review your resume as part of their service.

Resume Tip 3: Look at other people's Resumes

Have you ever seen anybody else's resume?

Many people may never have seen anybody else's but their own.

It is a very useful exercise to look at other people's resumes. Do they look like yours? Which do you prefer? Who would you employ?

The more resumes you can look at the better. Learn from each one and change yours accordingly.

Resume Tip 4: Google is your friend!

There is more information than you could ever read about resumes and interviews on the internet. Have you taken the time to read any of it?

Google is your friend – it can tell you all you need to know about writing a winning resume.

There are lots of example resumes as well as resume templates that you can use.

It is a good idea to research specifically for information relating to the industry you are applying for i.e. if you want to become a teacher; google "teacher resume".

Resume Tip 5: Use LinkedIn for Resume 'inspiration'

Hopefully you are already registered on LinkedIn. If not, why not?

For those not in the know, LinkedIn is like a Facebook for work colleagues. One of the key ingredients to a successful career is good networking.

There is some truth in the saying:

"It is not what you know but who you know."

Get yourself on LinkedIn as soon as possible and add everyone that you ever meet in the world of work. It is a great way to keep in touch with people and I guarantee you that one day one of those people will help you to get a job.

Another use of LinkedIn is to get inspiration for your resume. Many people upload their entire resume to LinkedIn and it is openly visible for anybody to look at. So search for people who work in the industry you are applying for and see if there are any good lines you could use in your own resume.

Search for people you have worked with in the past. Is their description of the work you did together better than the description you have used in your resume? If so use their description as 'inspiration' for your resume.

Resume Tip 6: Tailor your Resume to the job description: include KEYWORDS

The last tip I will give you regarding your resume is to tailor it to the job description.

Do not send the same resume out to every job application!

Lots of companies use recruitment agencies when they are taking people on. They provide the agency with a job description which the agency use in their advertisement.

Quite often the agency may have very little knowledge of the industry that they are recruiting for and may not even understand a lot of the terminology.

The way many of them select the most appropriate resumes to put forward to the company is by the use of KEYWORDS. Say for example the company have told them that they want somebody that has experience of using Microsoft Excel and Microsoft Word.

Once all the resumes are in, they will do a master search of the resumes for the keywords 'Microsoft Excel' and 'Microsoft Word'. If these words are NOT in your resume, it will not even be read.

If for example your resume says "vastly experienced in the use of Microsoft Office" – your resume may not be picked out even though you have the required experience, just because it doesn't include the keywords 'Microsoft Word' and 'Microsoft Excel' in.

So you must read the job description and make sure that the keywords that the agency may search for are included in your resume.

Let me be clear here, I am not telling you to add things to your resume that you do not have experience of, I am telling you to make sure that if you DO have the required experience – make sure the CORRECT words are in the resume, clearly stated – so that a simple search tool will not miss your resume.

Don't assume that agencies read each resume – they don't!

Chapter 19: A Great Resume Can Get You An Interview

A very crucial step for you in the job process is making sure that you have a resume that is going to stand out and catch the eye of the prospective employer. Below are a few suggestions on things you can do to help ensure you will have a better chance at positive results in acquiring the job that you are after.

1) A Great Resume Will Open the Door. The way to open the door that can lead you towards your dream job is to put together a great resume. If your resume demonstrates that you have made valuable contributions and accomplishments you will have a good chance of being granted an interview. If you are someone that has trouble tooting your own horn and perhaps do not have great writing skills then you should think of hiring a professional resume writer.

2) Brief Phone Interviews. Nowadays first interviews are frequently done over the phone even if you are a local candidate. Make sure to listen carefully to the questions being asked and then answer them as briefly and concisely as possible. The interviewer does not want the long drawn out version they are usually just wanting to confirm what your resumes suggests. It is a good idea to have some samples ready to backup the claims you have made on your resume.

3) Making the Right Impression. Companies have a variety of dress codes it is important to find out how your prospective employer wants you to dress for an interview. If the company has a business-casual dress code they may want you to wear a suit and tie for the interview. The best rule of thumb is not to assume but ask.

4) Focus on Interviewer's Questions. Depending on whether the job candidate

is listening and answering questions properly the interview is usually won or lost in a matter of minutes. If you bring your own agenda to an interview focus on the interviewer's questions first.

5) Maintaining Personal Integrity. Employers want to make sure that what you say in your resume match up with what you actually do. Do not put information in your resume that you cannot backup. Be careful not to oversell your experience.

6) Know Your Strengths & Weaknesses. You are not going to know everything about the company for your interview but make sure to articulate what your strengths are. We all have weaknesses so be prepared to discuss your weaknesses with the interviewer.

7) Rehearsing Interview Topics. If for example you have been fired or layed off previous jobs or have had long gaps between employment this would be a

good topic to rehearse what you are going to say to the interviewer.

8) Describe How You Will Contribute. Give samples of past contributions you have made to give your interviewer an idea of the types of contributions you can make to the company. Instead of focusing on your individual contributions express how you will be able to contribute to the company team. Showing that you are a team player. It is important that you are able to express what you have done to help a business move forward.

9) Research Appropriately. Try using LinkedIn as a research tool to learn a bit more about the people that will be involved with your interview process. Do not make the mistake of sending them an invite from LinkedIn as some may see this as creepy and it could affect the outcome of your interview.

10) Proper Business Questions. To demonstrate that you have done your research on the prospective employer is

by asking questions. They should focus on what you have learned about the business through your research. Perhaps have some questions specifically for the hiring manager to get to know them as you could be spending eight hours a day with this person.

11) Interview the Interviewer. You must interview the prospective employer just as they are interviewing you. Ask questions that will help you to determine what the style and expectation of the prospective employer is. Try and found out from other employees what the employer is like to work for.

12) Do Not Put the Interviewer on the Spot. Do not press the interviewer for an immediate assessment of your interview. Show that you are clearly interested in the job. Ask questions to gather information not to put the interviewer on the spot.

13) Stay Focused Throughout the Interview. Do not assume that the job is yours and get too comfortable in the

interview do not let your guard down but stay focused throughout the interview.

Follow Up. After your interview it is a good idea to send a thank you note or email to thank the people who were involved with your interview process. Try getting business cards from all of them so that you spell their names right. Lastly try not to forget anyone that was involved with the interview process.

Finding Your Dream Job. When you walk into an interview room 80% of the work has already been done you need to find the right words in about two sentences why you are the right person for this job. Do some research before hand to find out exactly what the hiring manager is looking for? If you know anyone in the company this could help, as 99% of the job candidates don't know anyone. You need to use everything that you have got to make you stand out from the rest of the crowd.

Persuade the Hiring Manager to Hire You. Do not tell but show the hiring manager that you have direct experience in the work you would be doing in the job. Bring documents or samples of previous work projects of yours to show the manager that you can solve his/her problem. Making sure that you understand exactly what the companies needs are is very important to helping you land the job.

Free Work to Build Portfolio. Doing free work with an employer or company can be good as it can help you to land the dream job that you want. This can help to open doors for you by agreeing to hire you themselves after a certain time period or to refer you to someone else. Make sure that you explain to the employee that you normally do not work for free and tell them what your normal rate is. Then suggest that you are willing to waive your fee for a two-week period to show them that you are the right person for the job. After the two-week period you can discuss going to your normal pay rate. By using this phrase or a similar one will help to ensure that you are not being taken advantage of.

Networking is one of the Most Important things You Can Do for Your Career. Instead of throwing your business cards at everyone locate people who are doing your dream job. Go to LinkedIn to locate people that are doing your dream career. Do some research on them and find out how they came to land the dream career they are in. After researching about them send them an email and slowly get to know them and eventually they will be able to give you some valuable advice on how to obtain your dream career.

Chapter 20: Making First Impressions

The interview doesn't necessarily start after you've settled in a seat across from the interviewer; it starts within the first few seconds of them laying their eyes on you. These few seconds are quite crucial, as your appearance and overall vibe can really make your interviewer get a glimpse into your personality and traits. This might not seem realistic until you think about how many people the interviewer might be meeting on a day-to-day basis to recruit. If your resume was all that was needed to land you your dream job, the meet-up would probably not have been an integral part of recruiting. Even though you might have an impressive resume, your personality can really make or break the deal. Even though you might have sat down the night before the interview to scroll through a couple of articles on what to do, wear, or even say during an interview, it can't guarantee that you'd ace it. Here we're answering questions you probably didn't ask the internet.

Smile

Can you think back on all those interviews you sat through with fidgeting hands and all the stuttering while your interviewer sat with a poker face and an intimidating voice? Don't worry; you weren't the only one! If only there was someone back then to tell you it could've all been avoided by one conscious effort: Smiling. The interviewer most probably has the experience and training to assess you almost instantly as you enter the space where your interview is being held. What if I told you, that you could also, almost instantly, set a positive tone for the duration of your interview with a genuine smile? It not only exudes great confidence, but a smile has also proven to make you feel that confidence too. When you show up with a smile on your face, it is almost always returned with a smiling face. This not only helps to create a relaxed environment, but it can also help you feel calmer when responding to intimidating questions. It can also help you overcome any blunders you might make by smiling in embarrassment and moving on, rather than getting stuck and potentially stuttering through the remaining interview.

A genuine smile can really make you seem more pleasant and approachable. It also lets the interviewer feel like you are eager to join the company and are happy to be given the opportunity to do so. However, steer clear of trying to force a smile! A fake smile is almost instantly spotted and can really have a negative impact. Try to stay calm and confident so that your smile comes from within.

Look in the Eyes

Just like smiling, looking in the eyes of your interviewer is also a sign of confidence. It can go hand in hand with smiling because if you're smiling but aren't able to make eye contact, the smile won't be able to work build to exuberate confidence. And if you're looking in the eyes of the interviewer without an occasional smile, it might make it super awkward for them. It can also make you seem less friendly. Constant eye contact doesn't only mean you're confident; it also shows that you are genuinely interested and focused. It lets the person feel that you are still with them rather than zoning out while they speak to you. However, moderation can be key here; it is not necessary to keep eye contact throughout the interview. You can look away while thinking about your response, or when you take a pause. If there is more than one person taking your interview, you can direct your eyes towards the person who asked you the question. If you are generally speaking to them all instead of a specific person, you can shift your gaze between them. Steady eye contact can really let the interviewer know that you are not trying to hide anything and that you are ready to answer any or all questions with confidence.

Make the First Move

The most common way to start the interview would be to let the interviewer initiate; however, it makes a more positive impact if you just go ahead and make that first move. As soon as you enter the space and make eye contact with your interviewer, walk towards them with a smile and an extended hand. Go on and introduce yourself rather than waiting for them to ask you or maybe look at the resume in hand and address you. It isn't just another way to show your confidence; it also lets them know that you are a pleasant and approachable person who can seamlessly strike a conversation in social circles and workplaces. It can also let the interviewer know that you could be a potential leader as well as a good team player. Once the interviewer initiates and leads the conversation, it can be very difficult to shift the tone of the interview. When you make that first move, it expresses your eagerness to be there, rather than be dreading the whole meeting. You are also able to set a tone that might help you to not only answer their questions but also give you the boost to ask a few yourself, another integral component of a successful job interview.

A Positive Handshake

As straightforward and simple as it might sound, a handshake can be a tricky business! For starters, you might be thinking that a handshake is such a basic etiquette, why is it even mentioned here? And why are we even calling it a positive handshake? Ask yourself how many people you come across who actually extend their hands to greet you with a handshake, 2 out of 10 maybe? It doesn't sound so basic anymore, does it? A handshake is a small gesture with a huge impact. A handshake can make you "click" with your interviewer and help you to build a connection with them subtly. Now talking about a positive handshake, yes, it is a real thing! Believe it or not, but there are handshaking etiquettes and are very rarely followed. It can lead to a disappointing first impression, which can become difficult to deter afterward. After

a bad handshake, you'd need to have the skills of a genius and a personal genie with a few wishes to spare, to be able to land that job.
For starters, never have a wimpy handshake using just your fingers. Your hand should firmly be placed palm to palm. You should have a gentle but firm hold, always avoid a bone crushing hold. The perfect handshake lasts a few seconds, which means two to three pumps up and down. Yes, there are people who sway their hands from side to side, which shouldn't be counted as a handshake. Another point to keep in mind is to make sure your hands don't sweat, or if they have a tendency to do so, always keep a handkerchief in your pocket. Wipe your hands with it before extending your hand. A sweaty palm can really be a pet peeve for some, and you don't want to take the risk of finding out if your interviewer is one of those people.
Always pair your handshake with a positive smile and a pleasant greeting.

Stay Relaxed, Confident and Enthusiastic

It might sound ridiculous to be told to try staying relaxed and enthusiastic during an interview, but you might think differently once you understand the importance of staying calm. Your nervousness and jittery nerves will show through regardless of how much you try to hide it. It is very important to relax and enjoy the interview. You probably spent a few hours for a few days before your interview trying to prepare for it, and are more than ready for it! Keep reminding yourself that! All you need to do is try to tell yourself you are ready, and that you can power through! Once you start believing in yourself, you can convince others to believe in you too. And there is nothing more confident than a relaxed candidate who knows what they are talking about. Your positivity and confidence will also let the interviewer know that you are not easily intimidated and truly believe in your skills and craft. However, confidence does not need to be accompanied by pompousness. There is a fine line between telling them you are a 'good fit for the job' and that you are 'too good of a fit for the job that the company wouldn't survive long without you' the latter will cost you the job you considered yourself too good for.

Remember Names

Have you ever met with an acquaintance or an old friend who couldn't seem to remember your name? Do you remember how it made you feel? Unimportant and irrelevant? Now imagine going to an interview, dressed well, prepared well, ready for any and all questions. But what if you can't remember the name of a relevant person during the interview, or even worse, the interviewer. It can be a deal-breaker not to remember relevant names as it can make the interviewer think you have a careless attitude or a non-serious nature. However, if you do a little research on the company and remember names relevant to your job or your field, it can really put quite an impression. Always make sure you study on the potential job and the company before showing up for the interview as it can really help you bag your dream job.

Your Body Language

The interviewers will not only focus on what you say but how you say it too. According to a research by the recruitment agency Cognitive Groups, 7% of your interview results depend on what you say. 38% on how you say it and a surprising 55% depends on the non-verbal aspects! Now those are big numbers that get very little attention. Non-verbal gestures include your facial expressions, your body language Following are a few rules, tips and tactics to help you get your body do the right kind of talking:

Open up yourself while sitting. Don't slack or sit with your arms closed at your chest. This shows you are trying to protect yourself. Sit in an upward position, slightly leaned forward with your hands folded on the table or in your lap. This shows confidence, openness, and interest in what the interviewer has to say to you.

Don't keep fidgeting in the chair or playing with the corners of your dress, your buttons, or your jewelry. These are all signs of nervousness. Even if you feel getting a little anxious, try taking deep breaths to calm your nerves down. Even if the nervousness comes through and your interviewer asks, 'Are you nervous?' Just be honest and accept the offer for a glass of water to take a few deep breaths. It is alright, they have all been there and wouldn't hold it against you unless you are open about it and not fidgeting or acting up.

Hand gestures are a good way to emphasize certain points, but only when done right. Keep the hand gestures steady and limited. Avoid pointing fingers or aggressively moving your hands around. Keeping your palm upwards suggests what you are saying is trustworthy. Steepling is a sign of confidence while touching your heart suggests what you are saying is genuine.

A good rule of thumb is to mirror your interviewer. Use the same kind of vocabulary, gestures, volume, and position as that of your interviewer. You should do this very subtly, of course. People generally trust those who are similar to them.

Chapter 21: Case Questions

If you know your boss is one hundred percent wrong about something, how do you handle it?

An employer asks this question to assess how you handle difficult situations and also to see if you have ever experienced difficulties working with a boss. Their main interest is to see how you describe your relationship with your boss.

It is one of the trickiest questions, and you should tread carefully when answering. You want to show that you are tactful when dealing with people; thus, you know just how to point out other people's errors depending on who it is.

You should avoid pretending that it has never happened. It sounds unrealistic that you have never corrected a boss, and that you do not think independently.

Explain it as a rare situation and let them hear how you addressed it diplomatically. Use an example to explain just how the situation occurred. You do not want to appear as the employee who is always questioning their employer; therefore, your example should be drawn from an element that affected the ability of your team to work effectively.

For instance, you could say, A while ago my boss assigned my team a project. I knew that the methodology she directed us to use was outdated and that there was a more current method. Knowing that this would affect our results, I privately went to her office and informed her. She thanked me and updated the information, and that gave us an immense boost.

Give an example of a difficult work situation that you overcame successfully.

This inquiry is a behavioral one that seeks to bring out how you respond to difficult situations, but most especially, how you deal with pressure. You want to impress your interviewers by showing them your ability to handle situations professionally and productively, ultimately achieving a resolution.

It is recommended that you use the STAR method to describe what the Situation was, the Task you undertook, the Approach you took to complete the task, and then explain the Results of your work.

Avoid speaking of yourself in a superior light or mentioning your own shortcomings.

An example that could be used here is one that has to do with dealing with problematic team members. Talk of how you engaged with them, made tough decisions, and achieved considerable success with your actions. You could also talk about being in a project that demanded exceptional performance under a tight deadline.

For instance, On one Friday afternoon at my former place of work I received an urgent call that had a query about a project I was working on. Unfortunately, my boss wasn't around as she had already left the workplace, yet she liked handling such sensitive queries directly. I managed to speak with the client about it, and I was able to work out a fairly good answer that could hold on until Monday the following week. The client was happy, and I also left a note to inform my boss about the call, and she was also happy.

Can you describe a situation in your life that makes you prouder than anything else?

The person conducting the interview is asking this because they want to hear about your great accomplishments! This is the time for you to brag about yourself a little bit so that they can see that you are the one for the job. Make sure to choose an accomplishment that shows off your character or your relevance to the job. If you are incredibly proud of your massive shoe collection, that's great, but it's not going to make you look good in the interview. Here's something you might consider stating instead:

I would have to say that I am proud of my dedication. It allowed me to go to school full-time while also working as a part-time intern to help advance my career a bit further. I'm proud of myself for putting in the hard work because it's certainly paid off so far!

Can you describe a time when you really learned your lesson, or had an enlightening moment that you still frequently apply to your current life?

The person conducting the interview is not going to expect that you are perfect. What they will be the most concerned about is that even if you do have a flaw, you know exactly what you need to do to fix it. They want to know that whatever issues you might have, you have the ability to recognize what needs to be learned from the situation and that you had learned the lesson. Life is not about regretting your mistakes; it's about learning from them. Here's what you might say:

There was one time when I found myself very stressed out from work on Friday to the point that I couldn't enjoy my weekend because I had so much to do on Monday. I had a fun trip planned that was completely ruined by my anxiety over work on Monday. I learned that it was most important for me to get my work done on time so that I could enjoy my time off work more.

Give an example of a time you were faced with a heavy workload and how you went about it.

It is always safe to expect questions about how you managed responsibilities on your previous job. Almost all job positions have times when the work piles up; hence, your answer helps the employer determine if you are a good match for the position.

The employer is most obviously seeking to employ someone who can respond effectively to workload increase without causing unnecessary drama. Avoid talking about that heavy workload as if you are blaming someone unless, perhaps a colleague who was on leave. Focus on explaining your achievement in meeting the workload. Avoid drama in your explanation, which will only show how you were stressed over a one-time unforeseen workload.

For instance, you could say, While in my previous job, a colleague of mine had completed a project to a certain client and then went on leave. The client happened to call while my colleague was on leave and requested to urgently amend some detail that had an error previously missed. I was able to fit in some extra time to stand in for my colleague and work on the client's corrections to keep her happy, while still ensuring to complete my other projects on time.

Explain one conflict that you faced at your previous place of work and how you handled it.

Employers pose this query to assess your dispute management styles to see how fast you are going to resolve issues should they arise in the course of your work. The question offers an insight into your behavior, interpersonal skills, and overall capability to manage conflicts.

Coming up with a positive example of a conflict can be daunting, especially in the interview situation, but you can apply the STAR method in describing a difficult work situation. Describe the Situation and Task in question, the Action taken, and the positive Results.

The worst thing you can do while you answer this query, however, is blast negative anecdotes on the individual or situation with which you had to deal.

Choose a genuine example, state categorically how you addressed it, and keep the story precise by only sharing the relevant details.

For instance, a colleague who was assigned to a project on our team began showing up late and it affected his ability to work, yet we were on a very tight deadline. I confronted him about it, and he became furious with me. However, I remained calm and explained the importance of arriving to work early. I vowed to help him figure a more convenient means of getting to work, and since then, he has not missed a day or showed up late again. He thanked me and we have worked productively ever since.

Tell me about a time you had to apologize to a friend or family member, and how you were able to rectify the situation.

This can be a pretty tricky one to answer, but there are times that it has been asked in an interview. The point is not to shame you or call you out. What they are looking for is your ability to take accountability. Can you admit when you are wrong? Can you acknowledge other people? Do you understand the various perspectives around a situation? Of course, don't share the most dramatic fight you've ever had, but don't be afraid to be honest! Let them really know what happened and show that you can take responsibility for things. Here's what you might say:

There was one time when I was on a trip with my Mom and sister. My Mom believed that we should go south to get to a restaurant, and I thought we had to go north. She insisted she checked, but I believed that I was right based on what I remembered from before. Turns out, she was right. I apologized and learned that I should always double check before I assume that I'm certain. Not only did I make myself look silly, but I invalidated my mother's intelligence.

Give a time when you went above and beyond the requirements of a project.

Interviewers ask this question to decipher your willingness to go over and above for your employer, even without being prompted to do so. Every firm wants to ascertain that, occasionally, you will do more than the norm just to get your job done.

Your goal when answering is to show the interviewer that you can do more than just the minimum job requirements. Show them that you can respond appropriately to a situation where your employer has a need that goes beyond your daily routine tasks.

Describe an example where you went beyond your job description to achieve a project goal. For instance, you might have transformed a process or taken the initiative of doing something your boss would do.

Be confident and focus on the quality of the task and indicate what you learned from the story.

However, do not exaggerate since the main point of focus here is to be believed.

For instance, in my previous job, I was working on a project for which I'd been provided the minimum requirements. I knew immediately that the project would eventually fail, even if my boss was satisfied at first. I decided to refine the project, which meant that I had to work on it from home on weekends.

What was your biggest failure?

While it may look like a no-brainer to put your focus on your strengths, addressing your difficulties can pay off better than you think. Employers want to know about your ability to own up to your own mistakes, about finding a resolution, and about your resilience by showing how you bounced back and grew from the experience. They obviously want to hire someone they are assured will contribute to their company by getting a realistic picture of you.

Any situation that you describe should be one which you assumed full ownership of your mistakes and took effective measures to not just fix the problem but also prevent it from occurring ever again. While you should be honest, avoid sharing something that could possibly ruin your chances of being employed and that which put the company in jeopardy. Most importantly, avoid putting blame on anyone else.

A good example to share is how you withheld an idea you knew would help improve a project's results in your previous job, and that it taught you to be more vocal and confident about your ideas in the workplace. Such can indicate that your failures could actually help you become a better employee. Even as one of the world's most famous entrepreneurs, Bill Gates, once said, It is okay to celebrate success, but it is also important to regard lessons learned from failure.

Chapter 22: Interview Parts

Job interviews are made with the necessary parts. It is not done randomly so as to avoid both the interviewer and interviewee confused with what they are talking about. It is best that you keep full attention to prevent you from asking too many questions. Always keep in mind that each interview has different parts. It helps you understand what you are asked to answer. On the part of the interviewer, it also makes him understand each answer from you. The process made in following the parts of the interview leads to a smooth-flowing job application thus it does not also mean that the style of interview others had can be applied to you. Applicants are different individuals with different personalities. Styles may be different but following the four basic parts of an interview is necessary!

Basic Parts of an Interview

Introduction – it is best if you can give the interviewer a positive note about you if you want to be accepted for the position. There is a quote that says, "First impression lasts". It is true especially when you are going through an interview.

Tips:

-Dress-up as a professional – you have to look good and fresh for your interview. You need to have that glow on your face when you enter the room as it reflects a strong personality. It is important that the interviewer gets stunned with how you carry yourself from the very first step you made going to the table.

-**Show enthusiasm** – you should catch the interviewer's attention by showing how enthusiastic you are to get the position. Do not do things in an over-acting manner as it might get the interviewer irritated with your actions and speech. Enthusiasm can be seen when you present yourself in a smart way and with enough energy.
-**Good manners** – from the time you are

seen, your manners are the ones being noticed in you. It is good to behave just with the right manners.

-Good communication skills – you are monitored with the way you talk. It is not helpful that your voice trembles and your hands shake while talking. Keep relaxed and confident.

Background – this helps the interviewer to take a deeper look of how you took and responded to the questions. It helps in determining about the basic qualifications you have or if you really have them at the very first step of the interview.

Tips:

-Handle yourself in the proper way – answering questions about your background may be very basic but it counts towards the interview process. Job applicants who handle and carry themselves the way they should for interviews get the bigger chance to come back for the next schedule and be accepted after few weeks.

-**Answer confidently** – all of your answers are counted in. Give them fast and meaty answers. It is either they stop the interview and immediately tell that you don't qualify or they may ask you more questions that might make your mind rattle and confused. Short but complete sentences always help. You should pick only the significant details in giving your brief background to the interviewer.

Discussion_- this is the part of your interview in which your communication skills is put to a test. Give it your best as you can make it with flying colors by just showing simply who you are and your humble but smart beginnings.

Tips:

-Show them what you've got – it is important to show you have the will to apply for the position. You must show that you are privileged and honored that you were called for the interview. Give them the best you have. Show them you have better things to offer compared to other applicants. Always remember that you are not the only one who needs a job. Every applicant is doing their best to land a job. It is time to shine out and have that confidence. You can do it in selling everything you've got in a strong manner.

-Ask and clarify – this is the time when you are given the chance to ask questions about the information you received during the process. This step makes the company determine if you are the one they are looking for to match the position they are offering. Do not be shy. Ask the right questions and you are guaranteed to have good answers and the company determines everything that is about your job application.

Close– every interview comes to an end. The interviewer usually ends it with few sentences. It is done very quickly, but you are always asked if you still have your final questions. You now see how the company wants everything to be clarified.

Tips:

-Avoid misunderstanding - the company wants everything clarified to avoid misunderstanding. It does not want your time to be wasted. They understand your concerns. Assessment of the interview at the end is important so you can think of the remaining questions you have to ask the interviewer.

-Last few questions – you were given the chance during your discussion to ask questions. Although you are also allowed in this last part of the interview to ask final questions, it does not mean that you have to ask as many as you can. One to three questions is enough so wrapping-up your interview will be quick. Job applicants are still waiting for their turn. The day cannot be spent with you alone. Make your final question relevant. It is perfectly fine that you were able to ask all the questions you have in mind during your discussion with the interviewer.

You should expect these basic parts of the interview to come out. It is better to be equipped with the best tips before going to your interview. The tips make you stronger. It shields you from getting pressured. Take the steps and remember them for a hassle-free interview very soon!

Chapter 23: The Keys To Success

Be Thorough With Your Experience and Skills

Focus on the area where your aptitudes are the strongest. Knowing these will help you tell your questioner why you deserve to get the job at hand.

Practice portraying your uncommon abilities and aptitudes.

Examine your work and instruction background. Search for aptitudes and encounters that match the set of responsibilities.

Keep Some Personal Experiences For References

Employers need genuine samples of how you have been and perform professionally. Recount to them a short story about your previous work experience.

Identify cases that represent where and how you have performed well utilizing your abilities and foundation, and relate them to the occupation for which you are applying.

Relate Your References To The Job Concerned

One of the best methodologies to state an experience is using the STAR (Situation-Task-Action-Result) approach. This approach allows you to explain the whole situation in a comprehensive yet concise manner. In your description, also include a statement about your learnings from the situation. Also, ensure that you do not make any scripted statements as your interviewers would have heard them a lot of times.

Early arrangement of musings and rehearsal of the same will help you to feel sure and convey unmistakably at the time of interview. Have the capacity to portray your helpful aptitudes as a relatable point in terms of the event that your questioner is not a master in the field. Here is a sample situation to explain how this methodology works:

Situation: When I worked at the state library, a hefty portion of the books were not documented effectively.

Task: I was responsible for arranging books on three stories.

Action: I planned and proposed a new system to my manager. I then displayed the new strategy to the library partners at the following staff gathering and everybody helped in planning for the new preparing the system for arranging books.

Result: After that gathering, there were less lost books, and clients got some information about discovering missing books.

Mock Interviews Are Good Practice

Mock interviews are like practice tests that you take before the final examination. Besides preparing you for the big day, they allow you to assess you own self on the skills and aptitudes requires for the job. As a result, you will be able to see you preparation from the perspective of the interviewer. When you begin to realize this view, you can prepare better to present yourself better.

Conduct Based Interviews

Questions based on situations and behaviors can be extremely tricky. Therefore, it is absolutely essential to practice them well in advance. Besides, assessing you on hypothetical situations, the interviewers also assess you on your past conduct. Subjects for these sorts of inquiries include:

Innovative answers for issues

Disagreements and clashes with collaborators

Meeting or neglecting to meet due dates

Qualities of a group pioneer and characteristics of a colleague

Persuading somebody to acknowledge your thought or idea

Responding to feedback from a prevalent, associate, or cohort

Adapting to a wide mixture of individuals, circumstances, and/or situations

Seeing an issue as an opportunity or challenge to prove your own worth.

Chapter 24: Closing

There are a number of effective closing techniques which effective salespeople utilize. I am going to keep this simple and recommend you focus on a technique called "The Question Close."

Closing a sale effectively means overcoming objections and getting the prospect to commit to purchasing, usually through signing a contract or a cash exchange.

A very important part of closing the job interview is asking for the job.

An example of using a question to close a sale would be "In your opinion, does what I offer solve your need?"

Another example, my favorite for job interviews, would be "Don't you agree that I would be a valuable addition to this department?" Closing questions are the only questions in which you are looking for a yes or no answer. This question should be asked cheerfully and with a big smile.

Look them in the eyes when you ask this question and be silent. Do not be the next person to speak.

If their answer is no then you've got more communication to do about how you solve their need. Follow up with another discovery question. "Tell me more about why you hesitate to say I would be a good fit?"

If their answer is yes then ask for the job. "Great, should I start on Monday or would tomorrow be better for you?" This question is especially effective in small companies or if you are talking to the "big boss."

If you know that this is the first interview and there will be at least one more interview potentially with other people you might say "Great! So will you put me on the list for a 2nd interview?" Again, look them in the eyes and be silent.

You prepare for the next interview the same way. You will probably have at least one new person whose felt need you will have to uncover. In the 2nd meeting you will probably focus more on the new person. They are likely the decision maker. If you know you are talking to the decision maker then his or her felt need is the only one that matters in terms of you getting the job.

Chapter 25: Top Job Interview Questions

What pet peeves do you have?

This question might seem really out of place for a job interview. However, there's a lot that an interviewer can tell from your answer. They can tell if you get irritated quickly by the length of the list of peeves. They can tell how well you will fit in the company depending on if you hate being micromanaged and their style of management.

There are some articles out there that suggest that you shouldn't list any pet peeves. However, I'm not sure that that's the best advice. Everyone is annoyed by something and you shouldn't downplay your irritation. You'll sound false if you try to pretend that nothing bothers you. Tell the interviewer one, maybe two of your pet peeves.

However, you make this question work for you. You should pick something that isn't something you will commonly see in the daily life of your job. Things like saying that you hate working on team projects isn't going to help you get a job where you will spend some time working in a team.

Picking the pet peeve carefully will help them see your attitude. So saying something along the lines of, "I hate jerks that talk, but don't do anything. These are the kind of people that don't do their part on team projects. That's really annoying," can be perceived as a little negative and presumptive.

Instead of that kind of answer, you might say, "I dislike negative attitudes. Those attitudes don't really help anyone and can cause problems, especially for the person themselves. We should be focused on finding the solutions to these problems." This shows that you're focused on finding a solution instead of focusing just on the problem. The answer can show your positive attitude and help them see what you want to do. A good answer will give the interviewer another reason to hire you.

What is your expectation for your salary?

Getting asked about the salary is always a tough question. However, there's good news. This doesn't have to be a really tough question. Part of the Jigsaw strategy is looking up salary information. You'll want to know the typical rates that people use. You'll want to not talk about the number right away.

However, the different answers you can give will depend on the person that is asking the question. If HR asks you about this, then you'll want to ask about what their salary range is for the job. They'll have that information for you. You'll be able to say whether or not you are comfortable with that range.

If you're being asked this by the hiring manager, then this is going to be a little more tough, even though you will have still options. There's a saying that goes around, "the one says a number first loses." This isn't necessarily true, but you will want to try hard not to say it first. You might even want to have a similar approach like you did with HR. You might want to ask them about what the going rates are." Most hiring managers will start talking to you about what's going on.

Others will want to know how much you are going to cost them. They'll ask you about the requirements that you need. You can come back and tell them, "I'm looking for a challenge. I want to use my skills is activities like X, I'm certain that you'll have a salary that will be appropriate for this job and its challenges. What does the company usually have in mind for this kind of job?" This will probably surprise a couple of people and get them talking about the information. A couple other people will still want to hear your range.

At this point, you can come at them with, "This is a new kind of position for me. I'm not sure without seeing the compensation plan with all of the benefits. My last salary was around $55,000. This position seems a little bit above this, so I would expect the salary to reflect this."

Negotiating a salary is tricky. There are books on the subjects for the reason. They can help you with some more specific advice about how to handle the salary question. Remember that your response will reflect the strength and confidence you could bring as an employee. Try to stay calm and cool to show off just how great you would be.

What your values in the workplace?

Asking about the values you have in the workplace is similar to asking about what your work ethic is like. They want to know about the kind of person that you are and what really matters to you. Your answer should be about your values. They'll speak to your character, integrity, and work ethic. Keeping your answer positive will really help you with this question.

However, try to make sure that you're still tying all of your answers back into the work you would do. Even if you're a great person that supports the environment, they're not going to be that interested in that kind of value unless it ties directly into the kind of work that they do. A great answer to that your workplace values are pretty much the same ones you have at home and in your personal life. This shows integrity.

As an example, I would say, "I do what I say I'm going to do. I try to put others before myself. I follow up on the things I commit to."

There are other great answers that you can use that are along the lines of, "I always do the best that I possibly can for the employer that has hired me to do a job. I work as hard as if I was working for a customer. Customer or boss, they deserve the absolute best."

You should also have an understanding of the corporate values are from research that you've done about the company. You should try to pick and choose the values that best align with what the company also wants. This doesn't mean that you should lie about the values that you have just to match up with what the company thinks.

Their core values will have a major impact on the work life if you work with them. You should have an understanding of these values before you go into the interview. They'll help you decide whether this place will be a good fit for you. If the values aren't in line with yours at all, then you will be unhappy in this workplace.

When you speak about your values, the hiring manager will be able to get an idea of what kind of person you are, what it will be like to work with you, whether or not you are trustworthy, and why you might be a good pick for this job.

How much did you earn at your previous job?

This is an uncomfortable job in all of its forms. However, it is a common question that people ask at some point. It comes up pretty early on in the process, and you need to know how to deal with it when it does come up.

There are different people that will ask this question. You might hear this from human resources. In that case, they just want to know that you won't refuse the job offer over money. If you were making $20,000 more dollars at your last job, then you're pretty likely to not take the job offer. This is the kind of information they want to know about up front.

If you don't hear about it during the application process, then the hiring manager will probably bring it up. At this point, they still want to know if the company can afford you. There are some people that really don't want to release this kind of information. In that case, you should probably say something along the lines of, "Can you help me understand what you want to know? I'm not that comfortable talking about my past salary. It doesn't relate to this job that much.

There are other factors beyond just the numbers. I'd love to answer any questions that you have about my skills or qualifications for this job. I do think that this company is great. I'm excited to discuss the possibility to work here. If I'm a good fit for this job, then I believe that we'll be able to reach an agreement when it comes to the salary."

You can also avoid the question by asking them a question in return like, "What's the range for this position's salary?" Once you've heard it, you should assure them that the range is acceptable. If they made you an offer, you wouldn't refuse it because of the money. Don't avoid answering the question because it may make this job harder or impossible for you to get. However, if you answer the question like this, you'll be in a place to negotiate the salary. The process of this question and figuring out the salary overall is a little bit like a dance.

There's no one right way to deal with the situation. You'll have to look at your situation and adjust for whatever it throws at you. I personally don't believe that it's a big deal to tell them how much you made at your last job. You can do tons of research online and find out information about the average salaries for tons of jobs. It can also be easy to see that this job is a step away from the other job. What you made previously shouldn't affect what you're making with a new job.

For the most part, a position will have a range for the salary. They will not offer you pay outside of that range, even if your previous pay was below that range. If they do try to give you something low, then you'll have options.

There are lots of books out there to read about negotiating your salary. Make sure that you do some research on the information to help you get the most out of the situation. If you're positive throughout the process, then you're more likely to come out on top as a winner.

What aspects of your last jobs did you like or dislike?

This kind of question might seem nice and easy, but you shouldn't relax too much. This question can get into your strengths and weaknesses. If you aren't thinking hard enough, then you might trip yourself. Pick the stories that will help you sell your best points. Pick stories that will relate to the new job as well. They might be able to show where you were able to excel and go beyond what was expected.

Don't tell them things that you hated about your old job that will be a major factor in your new job. Instead, you should pick a story that shouldn't be too related to the current position that you are looking. Some easy things to pick are the commute, the hours, and the time you spend traveling.

However, you should stay positive and stay away from complaints about your boss or the coworkers. Even though you'll be talking about negative answers when you talk about what you disliked, but you'll have to keep your attitude up. Don't keep focused on the negatives. This will help you appear better in the minds of the hiring managers that you encounter.

An example of answer would go like this, "I liked the strong communication opportunities that were there when I was working. I was able to really get things to happen and be successful in those positions. When I didn't believe that I was as successful as I could be, that was when I disliked my previous jobs. I can't stand bureaucracy or people that stand in the way of the team's success." This answer shows that you are driven and focused on the success of the team as well as yourself. Those qualities are critical to jobs that you will be getting. Make sure that you try to get in some reasons why people will want you for this job.

What is the most common critique people have about you?

This is a fairly dangerous job that you should be watching for. This is a question that people ask to get at what your weaknesses are. It is also a way to see how well you take criticism when it is given to you. In order to work well, you have to be open to criticism. It helps you grow in your job and improve as a person.

When you are able to take criticism, you will be 'coachable' which means that people will be able to help you understand your role more easily. It's a very desirable category.

There are some answers to avoid in this situation like, "People usually don't give me criticism." That's impossible. You won't be able to go through life without stepping on a couple of toes along the way. There's almost always from for improvement in your life.

You can try to use humor to deflect this question, but those answers aren't going to get you that far. They are going to press you for a more serious answer.

Regardless of the angle that you try to hit with your answer, you're going to have to be careful with the answer. You'll want to use a big-picture strategy. Any criticism or weakness that you have, you don't want to imply that it affects your job performance. You will want to imply the opposite, actually.

To show you a personal example, I get criticized quite often for being impatient. It's a constant thing I hear. However, being impatient has positively impacted my professional life. It's something that I work on often, but I also help nourish it when it comes to my professional life.

Perhaps you are constantly told that you take things seriously. You can state that you are a serious person. While you do have a sense of humor, you really want to focus on getting the job done first and getting to the fun parts later.

Perhaps you are thought of as overly critical. You can spin it by saying that you are focused on details are the most important thing to you. You are focused on creating a fantastic end result. You are working on getting better when it comes to offering encouragement as well.

There are a lot of ways that you can work with the criticisms to show off the positive things that you will bring to the job.

What is your most significant accomplishment?

This is a really great question to get when you interview. This will allow you to really show off what makes you perfect for the job. Don't talk about accomplishments outside of work (including kids or climbing mountains). The focus on the answer to this question should be on work-related matters that you have excelled at.

For example, if your company was going bankrupt and you managed to save them from that, then that might be a good answer. However, if that event doesn't exactly match up with the kind of work that you would be doing, then you might not want to use that answer. It just won't do you a ton of good.

You will be able to use a brag book during this period. You can look at performance reviews and all the other events that you have done well with to find a story. This question is really calling for a story for an answer. Don't focus just on the end result when you explain what happened. Start with what the situation was, then move onto the actions that you took, and then talk about what the end result was. If you focus on just the end result, then you're really depriving the interviewer of being able to hear so much more about you.

By getting into more of the details, the interviewer will be able to see how your mind was working behind the scenes to deal with the situation. You can include the obstacles that you faced and how you dealt with them. If you can, use your brag book to support the story that you're talking about.

If you don't already know, brag books are a collection of documents that show when you've done a good job. They can include performance reviews, reference letters, complimentary emails, good examples of your work, award letters, and other things that may not fit on a resume. If the story you're talking about also earned you an award or a nice email, then you will include this when you go to the interview. This helps the interviewer really see that you did something worthwhile.

A good story for this question can really show your skills in creativity, critical thinking, and within the skills relevant to your job. These kinds of points can help make a strong impression so that the hiring manager will be more likely to consider you at the end of the day.

Conclusion

In conclusion, carefully planning and organizing the information you intend to share in the interview, as well as how you intend to share it, is critically important for job interview success. The role of the interviewer is to determine whether you can help the organization solve its problems and take advantage of opportunities. The interviewer is most likely more skilled in interviewing than are you, so it is incumbent on you to be prepared.

The most significant and challenging part is to prepare yourself mentally and psychologically about appearing in the interview. Your body language does half the job for you; therefore, you should be mentally prepared and not sound or look nervous or less confident. This does not mean that you expose yourself as an arrogant or over-confident person. Research a couple of general questions that are asked in every interview and prepare you beforehand. Dress most appropriately according to the type of job you are applying for rather than an uneasy ill-fit wardrobe so that you do not lose on confidence due to consciousness. Be true to yourself and answer questions with the correct and crisp usage of words, reflecting your control over speech and though-process.

Thus, prepare this checklist before you appear for an interview, and you will come out with flying colors and thus sustaining an excellent respectful image in the eyes of the organization, which will boost your confidence further as well.

www.ingramcontent.com/pod-product-compliance
Lightning Source LLC
Chambersburg PA
CBHW072002070526
44583CB00015B/1295